The gourmet's guide to
Italian Cooking

The gourmet's guide to
Italian Cooking

Sonia Allison and Ulrike Bielfeldt

OCTOPUS
Octopus Books

First published 1973 by
Octopus Books Limited
59 Grosvenor Street London W1

ISBN 0 7064 0086 0

©1973 Octopus Books Limited

Produced by Mandarin Publishers
77a Marble Road North Point Hong Kong
and printed in Hong Kong

Contents

The flavour of Italy

The flavour of Italy is abundant freshness and, because this country is blessed with an enviable climate, one is warmly welcomed by a profusion of aromatic basil, sage, rosemary, marjoram, thyme, mint, parsley and bay. Sweet, sun-ripened tomatoes which drip with juice. Delicate, champagne-gold olive oil. Garlic and salami and Mortadella and heady wines. Crusty bread and pungent cheeses. Parma ham and ripe figs. Artichokes, honey-sweet melons and myriads of olives in green, black, purple and brown. Fleshy apricots, peaches, pears and cherries with grapes that taste like nectar. Wood strawberries and multi-coloured pimentos. Sweet-scented oranges and lemons. Exotic fish from sea and lakes. Saffron and white truffles and such a lavish array of fresh vegetables that every Italian street market looks like an Aladdin's cave.

What emerges from a study of Italian cuisine is the fact that it does not depend for its success on elaborate and rich sauces, on expensive and impressive additions and on ornate decorations and garnishes. Rather it is totally unpretentious, relatively uncomplicated, traditional, individual and, like the Italian people themselves, charming and utterly captivating. The food—be it a simple bowl of pasta shimmering with melted butter or a glass of warm zabaione—is always a pleasure and a joy to eat. The simplicity of style and presentation, coupled with the freshness and quality of the ingredients used, place it, without question, in the haute cuisine class. But looking back in time, this should come as no surprise, for the splendours of the early Roman banquets made history and, ever since, the Italians—who make no secret of their love of good food—have eaten and drunk handsomely and heartily and enjoyed every minute of it!

Now that Italian ingredients are more readily available everywhere, there is no reason why the rest of us should not share, with the Italian people, some of their own distinctive cooking. This book, containing a reasonable sprinkling of the kind of everyday dishes eaten in the average Italian home, should serve as a useful introduction to a style of food which, as early as the 16th century, was brought to the French Court by Catherine de Medici, the Italian wife of King Henry II of France.

Preparing the meal

Antipasti

Fanciful starters figure very little in the repertoire of Italian cookery. Instead it is more customary to have a small bowl of freshly cooked pasta crowned with Parmesan cheese or a traditional sauce. Or gnocchi, pizza or risotto. Mortadella sausage (a Bolognese speciality) with a dish of olives to go with it. Beef and chicken broth with pastini. Minestrone or the simple but unique stracciatella. Huge tomatoes grilled with tuna. A plate of bean salad. Raw mushrooms and anchovies tossed with the simplest of dressings. Mild ham and salami in all its varieties. Freshly fried sardines or local scampi. Bagna cauda with fresh vegetables. Ravioli. Nothing, you might say, particularly elaborate; nothing especially impressive —just eminently appetizing, which is surely what a good starter ought to be.

Antipasto misto   Mixed antipasto

4 oz. Italian salami, finely sliced
12 each, black and green olives
4 hard boiled eggs
1 small can anchovies in oil
2 oz. ($\frac{2}{3}$ cup) raw button
mushrooms, sliced
1 canned red pimento
3 oz. (1 cup) cooked green beans
(French or snap)
2 tablespoons (2½T) olive oil
1 tablespoon (1¼T) lemon juice
seasoning to taste
serves 4

A colourful mixed hors d'oeuvre which makes an appetizing and fairly substantial starter to a light meal.

Arrange the salami and olives on a long platter. Cut the eggs into wedges and stand on top of the salami. Drape the drained anchovies over the eggs.
Put the mushrooms into a bowl. Chop the pimento and add to the bowl with the green beans. Beat the oil, lemon juice and seasoning well together. Add to the mushroom mixture and toss well.
Arrange in small heaps round the edge of the platter.

Antipasto di peperoni e pomodori   Pimento and tomato antipasto

4 pickled red and
yellow pimentos
4 large tomatoes, skinned and
sliced
2 tablespoons (2½T) olive oil
1 tablespoon (1¼T) lemon juice
seasoning to taste
1 small onion, chopped
1 heaped tablespoon (1½T) finely
chopped parsley
serves 4

A gay and flavourful hot weather starter.

Cut the pimentos into strips and arrange on a platter, then top with tomato slices.
Beat the oil, lemon juice and seasoning well together and pour over the pimentos and tomatoes. Sprinkle with onion and parsley.

Melanzane ripiene   Stuffed aubergines (eggplants) with egg

2 medium aubergines (eggplant)
salt and pepper
olive oil
4 oz. (2 cups) fresh white
breadcrumbs
2 large hard boiled
eggs, chopped
8 green olives, stoned and
sliced
1 small garlic clove, crushed
8 anchovy fillets, chopped
squeeze of lemon juice
1 heaped tablespoon (1½T)
chopped parsley
1 level teaspoon marjoram

serves 4

The aubergine—or eggplant—established itself in Italy many centuries ago but despite its familiarity to the people of the country, it is used much less in Italian cuisine than other vegetables of lesser worth. Consequently recipes for it are scarce and those that do exist are surprisingly unimaginative. This version of Stuffed Aubergines is more interesting than most and is a tasty dish with anchovies, garlic, olives and egg adding the flavour interest. It may be eaten either hot or cold but in my opinion is best straight from the oven with crusty bread and red wine.

Preheat the oven to moderate (350°F, Mark 4). Wash and dry the aubergines (eggplant) and cut them in half lengthwise. Make gashes in the flesh with a knife then stand, cut sides uppermost, on an oiled baking tray.
Sprinkle with salt and pepper then brush fairly heavily with oil.
Cook in the centre of the oven for 30 minutes. Remove from the oven and cool off slightly.
Carefully cut out the flesh (leaving ¼-inch thick aubergine (eggplant) shells), chop finely and put into a bowl. Add all the remaining ingredients then season well to taste, but watch the salt as the anchovies will doubtless contribute their own share.
Return the mixture to the aubergine (eggplant) shells and sprinkle lightly with oil. Cook in the centre of the oven for a further 30 minutes.

Mixed antipasto

Mixed salads with mortadella
and salami *(left)*

Cauliflower salad *(below)*

Raw mushroom salad *(right)*

Asparagus on artichoke hearts
(below right)

Insalata di fagioli   Dressed beans

¾ lb. (2 cups) shelled broad,
lima or haricot beans
1 cut clove garlic
3 oz. (½ cup) lean ham,
finely chopped
3 tablespoons (3¾T) olive oil
3 dessertspoons (3T) lemon
juice or mild vinegar
seasoning to taste
½ level teaspoon dried or 1 level
teaspoon fresh basil

serves 4

A simple hors d'oeuvre for summer eating.

Cook the beans in boiling salted water until just tender and still crisp.

Meanwhile, rub the cut clove of garlic round the inside of a salad bowl. Add the drained beans and ham.

Beat the olive oil and lemon juice or vinegar well together with the seasonings. Add to the beans in the bowl and toss thoroughly to mix. Chill thoroughly and sprinkle with basil just before serving.

Alternatively, top the beans with a little mayonnaise, then garnish with anchovy fillets, rolled round black olives, and tomato slices.

Dressed beans

Crostini di provatura   Hot cheese antipasto

These are filling mouthfuls, simply made from fried bread and Bel Paese cheese. They must be served piping hot and are a pleasurable experience on bleak winter days.

Allowing 3 or 4 per person, cut de-crusted slices of white bread into small rounds or squares and fry in a mixture of hot olive oil and butter until crisp and golden on both sides.

Top each round or square with a slice of Bel Paese cheese then stand under a preheated hot grill. Leave until cheese just begins to melt then serve straight away.

Anchovies—so beloved by the Italians—are the traditional garnish but the antipasti are just as good without anything at all.

Insalata di riso   Rice salad

8 oz. (1¼ cups) long grain rice
2–3 tablespoons (2½–3¾T)
mild vinegar
2–3 dessertspoons (2–3T)
olive oil
seasoning to taste
nutmeg (optional)
1 level dessertspoon (1T) finely
chopped parsley
1 oz. (⅛ cup) flaked almonds or
pine nuts
2 oz. (½ cup) prawns
(shrimp), chopped
1 small red or green pimento,
de-seeded and chopped
1 medium celery stalk,
finely chopped
1 small onion, grated
green olives, or ham and
watercress for garnishing
serves 4

An easily prepared dish which may be livened up with any manner of additions, depending on what is in the refrigerator or store cupboard. Chicken may be substituted for prawns [shrimp], chopped cucumber for green pepper, walnuts for almonds and leek for onion. Capers may be added as well and so may lightly cooked green peas, cooked mussels, finely chopped ham and a hint of finely chopped fresh mint.

Cook the rice in about 1 pint (2½ cups) boiling salted water until tender; 12–15 minutes. Drain thoroughly. Add vinegar and olive oil and mix well with a fork. Season to taste with salt and pepper and, if liked, a grinding or two of nutmeg.
Stir in all the remaining ingredients (except the olives), then transfer the rice mixture to a lettuce-lined serving dish.
Garnish with olives or with rolls of ham and watercress.

13

Ham, tuna and fennel appetizer (left)

Parma ham with melon (below)

Raw vegetables with hot garlic sauce (right)

Carciofi   Globe artichokes

Cut the stems off the artichokes and remove the first two rows of leaves. Cut the tips off the remaining leaves with scissors. Soak the artichokes for 30 minutes in cold, salted water. Drain thoroughly. Stand the artichokes upright in a saucepan and add about 4 inches of boiling water and one level teaspoon of salt. Bring to the boil, lower the heat and cover the pan. Simmer gently for 30 to 40 minutes or until the leaves pull out easily. Drain very thoroughly by turning the artichokes upside down on to paper towels.

Serve hot with melted butter or cold with mayonnaise (see opposite) or salad dressing.

serves 4

Carciofi alla maionese   Artichokes with mayonnaise

Medium-sized, fresh and tender artichokes which, ideally, should be used for this dish are prolific in Italy but not so readily available elsewhere. Consequently one has to compromise and use either freshly boiled globe artichokes (see above)—the large leafy variety —or canned artichoke hearts instead.

If using the latter, allow 2 per person. Drain well on paper towels and stand on lettuce-lined plates. Coat thickly with mayonnaise then sprinkle with chopped hard-boiled eggs and the merest suspicion of freshly chopped basil or mint.

Artichokes with mayonnaise

Maionese   Mayonnaise

2 or 3 egg yolks (from large eggs)
½ level teaspoon salt
¼ level teaspoon white pepper
2 tablespoons (2½T) fresh lemon juice
½ pint (1¼ cups) olive oil

In Italy mayonnaise is widely used for all manner of dishes and in its simplest form is a mixture of the best possible olive oil—the finest is said to come from Lucca in Tuscany—egg yolks, lemon juice, salt and white pepper to taste. Occasionally a sparing amount of chopped garlic is added as well, as are finely chopped parsley and freshly chopped basil. For most general purposes, though, the mayonnaise is used without any additions at all.

Put the egg yolks, salt, pepper and 1 dessertspoon (1T) of lemon juice into a basin. Beat thoroughly. Gradually add half the oil, drop by drop, beating hard all the time.

When the mayonnaise is thick and glistening, add a further dessertspoon (1T) of lemon juice. Add half the remaining oil in a slow, steady stream, beating all the time. Beat in the rest of the lemon juice and oil.

Preparing mayonnaise
(a) The egg yolks, salt, pepper and lemon juice are beaten together thoroughly.
(b) Oil is added to the egg mixture drop by drop, beating hard all the time.
(c) Curdled mayonnaise can be rescued by breaking an extra yolk into a bowl and very gradually beating the curdled mayonnaise into it.

Adjust seasoning to taste, adding a dash of wine vinegar if the mayonnaise seems on the bland side. To stop separation, stir in a dessertspoon of boiling water at the very end.

The mayonnaise may be stored in a lightly closed container in the least cold part of the refrigerator or pantry for up to one week. Curdled mayonnaise is the result of adding the oil too quickly in the early stages. Should this happen—and not even expert cooks are immune—break a fresh egg yolk into a basin and very gradually beat the curdled mayonnaise into it.

a

b   *c*

Fondi di carciofi all'olio e aglio   Garlic dressed artichoke hearts

Make a dressing by beating 6 dessertspoons (6T) olive oil with 2 dessertspoons (2T) lemon juice and 1 dessertspoon (1T) wine vinegar. Season to taste with salt and pepper, then pour into a screw-topped jar. Add 1 large cut clove of garlic, cover and leave overnight.
Allow 2 or 3 canned artichoke hearts per person. Just before serving, stand them on a lettuce-lined plate. Shake the dressing thoroughly then pour over the artichokes. Sprinkle with chopped ham and serve straight away.

Fondi di carciofi con asparagi   Asparagus on artichoke hearts

4 artichoke hearts
4 eggs
2 lb. asparagus
Hollandaise sauce

Poach the artichoke hearts, then leave them to cool. Hardboil the eggs. Wash and scrape the asparagus and discard the tough part of the stalks. Tie in bundles and cook in boiling, unsalted water for 15 to 20 minutes.
Chop the eggs, mix with some of the asparagus tips and place on the artichoke hearts. Place the remaining asparagus tips on top and pour over Hollandaise sauce.

serves 4

Antipasto di pomodori e gamberi
Tomato prawn antipasto

4 large tomatoes
1 small onion, very finely chopped
1 oz. (2T) butter
4 oz. (1 cup) shrimps or prawns, finely chopped
½ oz. (¼ cup) fresh white breadcrumbs
4 anchovy fillets, finely chopped
1 level tablespoon (1¼T) finely chopped parsley
pepper to taste

serves 4

Preheat the oven to moderately hot (375°F, or Mark 5).
Cut the tops off the tomatoes, then scoop out the inside fibres and seeds and reserve these. Stand the tomatoes upside down to drain on soft kitchen paper.
Fry the onion gently in the butter until pale gold. Stir in the shrimps or prawns, crumbs, anchovies, parsley and salt and pepper to taste. Stir in sufficient tomato pulp to moisten the mixture. (Keep remainder for soup and stews.)
Return the mixture to the tomato cases. Cook just above the centre of the oven for 20 minutes.

Pomodori ripieni di acciughe   Anchovy stuffed tomatoes

4 very large tomatoes
8 anchovy fillets
1 oz. (½ cup) fresh white breadcrumbs
1 garlic clove
1 tablespoon (1¼T) olive oil
salt and pepper to taste
a little beaten egg
4 stoned green olives

Preheat the oven to moderately hot (375°F, or Mark 5).
Cut the tops off the tomatoes, then scoop out the inside fibres and seeds and reserve these. Stand the tomatoes upside down to drain on soft kitchen paper.
Finely chop the anchovy fillets and put them into a basin with the crumbs. Crush the garlic and add to the basin then stir in the olive oil. Season well to taste with salt and pepper then bind with a little tomato pulp (keep the remainder for soup and stews) and a little beaten egg.
Return to the tomato cases then top each with an olive or with the tomato tops. Cook just above the centre of the oven for 20 minutes. Garnish with parsley.

serves 4

19

Pomodori ripieni di tonno e capperi
Tuna stuffed tomatoes with capers

Prepare the tomato cases exactly as in the previous recipe.
To make the filling, combine 6 heaped tablespoons (8T) mashed tuna
with 1 level dessertspoon (1T) finely chopped capers.
Stir in sufficient mayonnaise both to moisten and bind the mixture.
Season to taste with salt and pepper, then return to the tomato cases.

serves 4

Sprinkle with finely chopped parsley and serve very cold.

Prosciutto con tonno e finocchio
Ham, tuna and fennel appetizer

4 slices lean ham
1 can (approximately 7 oz.) tuna
¼ pint (⅝ cup) mayonnaise
3 level tablespoons (3¾T) grated fennel
12 black olives
1 small red pimento, de-seeded and cut into strips

serves 4

Tuna, with its meaty texture and superb yet subtle flavour, combines
admirably with most other ingredients and, when teamed with
aniseed flavoured fennel and mild, lean ham, makes an intriguing
starter to a hot or cold meal.

Arrange the ham on a serving platter.
Drain the tuna and break the flesh into smallish chunks. Stand in a
line on top of the ham.
Combine the mayonnaise and fennel well together. Spoon over the
tuna then stud with olives and decorate with a criss-cross of pepper
strips.

Uova tonnate
Egg and tuna mayonnaise

lettuce
½ can (approximately 3½ oz. tuna
¼ pint (⅝ cup) mayonnaise
4 hard boiled eggs
8 anchovy fillets
serves 4

Arrange the lettuce leaves on 4 individual plates.
Drain the tuna thoroughly. Mash it finely then stir it into the
mayonnaise.
Cut the hard boiled eggs in half and stand 2 halves, cut sides down,
on each plate. Coat them with the tuna mixture, then garnish each
with anchovy fillets.

Antipasto di patate con tonno e peperoni
Potato antipasto with tuna and pimento

6 medium potatoes
3 tablespoons (3¾T) olive oil
3 dessertspoons (3T) lemon juice
salt and pepper to taste
1 can (7 oz.) tuna
¼ pint (⅝ cup) mayonnaise
1 medium onion, finely chopped
1 medium green pimento

serves 4–6

Wash and scrub the potatoes and boil in their skins until tender.
Drain and leave until cool enough to handle, then peel and cut them
into dice. Toss with oil and lemon juice and sufficient salt and pepper
to taste.
Drain the tuna and mash finely. Combine it with the mayonnaise and
onion. Add the potatoes and toss gently but thoroughly with a spoon.
Cut the stem off the green pimento, then remove the inside fibres and
seeds. Cut the pimento itself into rings and arrange on top of the
potatoes.

Tonno con faglioli
Florentine tuna and bean antipasto

1 cut garlic clove
1 can (7 oz.) tuna
3 dessertspoons (3T) lemon juice
1 teacup (½ cup) haricot beans, soaked overnight and freshly cooked until tender
salt and pepper to taste
serves 4

Rub the salad bowl with the cut clove of garlic.
Drain the tuna and beat the tuna oil with lemon juice. Pour into the
salad bowl and add French or snap beans and drained haricot beans.
Toss thoroughly and season well to taste with salt and freshly milled
pepper.
Flake the tuna and arrange in a mound on top of the beans.

Insalata di funghi Raw mushroom salad

12 oz. (3¼ cups)
button mushrooms
1 clove garlic
½ level teaspoon finely grated
lemon peel
3 tablespoons (3¾T) olive oil
3 dessertspoons (3T)
lemon juice
pinch of ground nutmeg
salt and pepper to taste
4 anchovy fillets, or parsley

serves 4

Morning-fresh button mushrooms are essential for the success of this starter, as only these have the delicacy of flavour so esteemed by epicures.
Wipe the mushrooms clean, then cut into thin slices.
Cut the garlic clove in half and rub it round the inside of a wooden or glass salad bowl. Add the lemon peel, oil, lemon juice, nutmeg and salt and pepper to taste. Beat thoroughly to mix.
Add the mushrooms and toss gently with a spoon until all the slices are coated with oil/lemon juice mixture. Cover and leave to stand at room temperature for 15 minutes.
Transfer to 4 individual plates and sprinkle the tops of each with thin slivers of anchovies or with chopped parsley.

Bagna cauda con crudita Bagna cauda with raw vegetables

3 oz. (⅜ cup) unsalted butter
5 tablespoons (6¼T) olive oil
1 small can anchovies in oil,
drained and chopped
2–6 garlic cloves, chopped
to serve
4 celery stalks, cut into
2-inch lengths
1 red pimento, cut into fairly
wide strips
1 green pimento
4 small carrots, peeled and cut
lengthwise into sticks
¼ small white cabbage, cut into
fairly wide strips
serves 6–8

A sophisticated but essentially simple starter from the Piedmont region. Basically bagna cauda is a buttery, garlic-flavoured hot sauce into which pieces of crunchy raw vegetables are dipped and then eaten. For those who can stomach rich, strong foods without suffering any after-effects, this Northern speciality is a worthwhile experience; however, those with more delicate digestions are advised to settle for something less potent!

Put the butter, olive oil, anchovies (plus their oil) and the garlic cloves into a saucepan and cook gently for 15 minutes.
Transfer to a heatproof dish standing on a spirit stove or electric plate warmer and serve the hot sauce accompanied by the raw vegetables.

Bagna cauda con panna Bagna cauda with cream

A more mellow-tasting version, but infinitely richer.
Make the bagna cauda as directed in the previous recipe. When it has cooked for 15 minutes, blend in ¼ pint plus 4 tablespoons (1 cup) double (heavy) cream, heated until hot.
Transfer to a heatproof dish and serve straight away.

Bagna cauda con panna e tartufi Bagna cauda with cream and truffles

Simultaneously with the cream, add 1 or 2 very thinly sliced canned white truffles.

note: bagna cauda may also be served as an appetizer with drinks.

Crostini di acciughe Hot anchovy antipasto

8 slices French bread, each
between ¼ and ½-inch thick
2 oz. (¼ cup) butter
2 tablespoons (2½T) olive oil
1 tablespoon (1¼T) melted butter
1 level tablespoon (1¼T) flour
¼ pint (⅝ cup) milk
1 oz. (¼ cup) grated
Parmesan cheese
salt and pepper to taste
8 anchovy fillets
2 extra level tablespoons (2½T)
grated Parmesan cheese
about 1 oz. (2T) butter
serves 4

A rich and satisfying starter with a memorable flavour.
Fry the bread in the hot butter and olive oil until crisp and golden on
both sides. Drain on soft kitchen paper then stand in the grill pan.
Heat the melted butter in a saucepan. Stir in the flour and cook for
2 minutes without boiling. Gradually blend in the milk. Cook,
stirring, until the sauce comes to the boil and thickens. Simmer for
2 minutes. Stir in 1 oz. (¼ cup) Parmesan cheese then season well to
taste with salt and pepper.
Spoon equal amounts over the fried bread in the grill pan then top
each with an anchovy fillet. Sprinkle the rest of the Parmesan cheese
over each, then dot with flakes of butter. Brown quickly under a hot
grill and serve straight away.

Salame con le olive Olive and salami antipasto

4 oz. Italian salami, very
thinly sliced
4 oz. (1 cup) Bel Paese or
Provolone cheese, cubed
4 large tomatoes, skinned and
sliced
2 dozen small black olives
1 red pimento
2 level tablespoons (2½T) finely
chopped parsley
1 tablespoon (1¼T) olive oil
1 dessertspoon (1T) lemon juice
salt and pepper to taste
serves 4

Cover a serving platter with salami then arrange cheese, tomatoes
and olives attractively on top.
De-seed the red pimento and cut it into thin strips. Put them into a
bowl with the parsley. Add oil, lemon juice and salt and pepper to
taste and toss ingredients well to mix.
Place, in mounds, on top of the antipasto and serve with bread sticks
and a robust red wine.

Prosciutto di parma con melone Parma ham with melon

A classic and famous dish from Parma, beloved by connoisseurs all
over the world. Parma ham, with its mild, delicate flavour and
colouring, owes its distinctive and unique qualities to curing
methods and climate and when combined with cool, honey-sweet
melon or fresh ripe figs, it makes one of the most superb starters ever
created. Like all good things, Parma ham is now very expensive so
one must be grateful that it is always served in paper thin slices and
in fairly sparing quantities!
There are two ways of serving Parma ham with melon.
One: cut a melon (sweet, ripe and preferably chilled) into 2–3-inch
thick slices and remove the skin and seeds. Allow one slice per
person and stand on a plate. Cover with 1 or 2 slices of Parma ham
and serve straight away.
Two: cut slices of melon into reasonably large cubes and wrap pieces
of ham round each. Secure with cocktail sticks (cocktail picks) then
transfer to a serving platter. Allow 4 to 5 per person.

Prosciutto di parma con fichi Parma ham with figs

Try this when fresh figs (purple skinned and red hearted) are
available. Simply cover plates with 2 or 3 thin slices ham per person
then stand 2 fresh figs on top. Eat both together.

Parma ham with melon

Soups

There are two main kinds of soup in Italy. The first are thick, minestrone-type affairs with pasta or rice and a miscellany of vegetables. The second are clear and thin beef or chicken broths, usually served with baby pasta or ravioli. In addition, one finds simple versions of tomato, mushroom, pea and spinach soups, certain regional specialities and unusually delicious zuppe di pesce or fish soups. No Italian soup is arduous to make. No soup is so rich that it is an effort afterwards to eat the main course. Maybe this is the reason why, in almost all Italian homes, soup is part of the daily pattern of life and enjoyed through all four seasons of the year.

Visitors to Italy in summer may be astonished, when they sit down to lunch in a hotel or restaurant, at being presented with large plates of steaming soup when all they want is something iced and fruity. It may seem like a touch of madness, but just as soup alleviates the cold of winter, so does it reduce the overbearing heat of summer. In fact, soup acts as a perfect insulation and for this reason it is worth going along with this old Italian custom.

Minestrone   Minestrone

If Italy is famous for one dish—apart from spaghetti—then surely it must be minestrone, the hearty vegetable and pasta (or rice) soup which is a speciality from the Northern regions, including Lombardy and Liguria. As with all traditional dishes, recipes for minestrone vary from family to family and even in cook books, few versions are identical. Therefore to give an exact recipe is a hard task, although I have attempted to keep the following three as authentic as possible. Italian housewives—for reasons of economy—make minestrone with almost any vegetables in season and if there is a glut of artichokes or aubergines (eggplant), then in it goes!

Minestrone Milanese   Minestrone Milanese

1 ham bone
1 large onion, chopped
2 medium carrots, diced
3 medium celery stalks, coarsely chopped
½ small head (3 cups) cabbage shredded
1 large leek, trimmed and chopped (optional)
3 pints (7½ cups) beef broth
2 oz. (approximately ¼ cup) dried haricot beans, soaked overnight
salt and pepper to taste
1 small marrow or squash, diced
4 oz. (⅝ cup) long grain rice
1 large potato, diced
1 garlic clove, finely chopped
1 level teaspoon fresh chopped basil or ½ level teaspoon dried
1 level tablespoon (1¼T) chopped parsley
grated Parmesan cheese
serves 6

Put the ham bone into a large saucepan with the onion, carrots, celery, cabbage, leek and beef broth.
Drain the haricot beans, then add to the pan with salt and pepper to taste. Bring the soup to the boil and remove any scum that rises to the surface. Cover the pan, lower the heat and simmer gently for 2¾ hours or until the beans are tender, adding a little extra water if the soup thickens too much.
Add the marrow or squash, rice, potatoes and garlic and continue to simmer for a further 20 minutes. Stir in the basil and parsley and serve very hot.
Accompany with cheese.

Minestrone Genovese   Genoese minestrone

1 breakfast cup (1 cup) loosely packed parsley
2 garlic cloves, chopped
a good shake of salt
1½ oz. (approximately ¼ cup) shelled walnut halves, chopped
2 oz. (½ cup) grated Parmesan cheese
3 tablespoons (3¾T) olive oil

This is minestrone soup with the addition of pesto, a green coloured flavouring with the consistency of butter. Italians make pesto themselves, often laboriously in a pestle and mortar, and add it not only to soup but also to pasta. Alas, in other countries, the essential ingredients may not be so easy to find and therefore we would advise either buying pots of pesto from Italian food shops or making a sort of substitute pesto with more familiar ingredients. The previous recipe for Minestrone soup will serve admirably and here is an adaptation of pesto.

Remove the parsley from the stalks and put into a large mortar. Add garlic, salt, walnuts and cheese.
Pound with a pestle until the mixture thickens to a paste-like consistency. Gradually work in oil, a drop at a time, and continue stirring until mixture is like soft butter. Stir about 2 tablespoons (2½T) (or more to taste) into the Minestrone.
Any left-over pesto should be put into a jar, covered with foil and stored in the least cold part of the refrigerator.

True Pesto
To make this, use leaves of fresh basil instead of the parsley, and pine nuts instead of the walnuts.

serves 6

Minestrone with shell pasta

Minestrone   Minestrone

2 tablespoons (2½T) olive oil
1 large onion, finely chopped
4 rashers lean bacon, chopped
(bacon strips)
1 small head (approximately
6 cups) white
cabbage, shredded
4 celery stalks, chopped
3 pints (7½ cups) beef stock
2 oz. (¼ cup) dried haricot
beans, soaked overnight
salt and pepper to taste
4 large tomatoes, skinned and
chopped
2 level tablespoons (2½T)
tomato concentrate
1 garlic clove, finely chopped
6 oz. (1 cup) any other
vegetables in season, such as
diced marrow, diced aubergines
or eggplant, cauliflower florets,
diced turnips, diced parsnips,
diced swedes, shelled peas or
sliced green or snap beans
2 oz. (½ cup) broken macaroni
1 level teaspoon dried basil
or thyme
grated Parmesan cheese
serves 6

Heat the oil in a large saucepan. Add the onion and fry very gently, with a lid on the pan, until soft but still white. Add the bacon and fry for a further 3 minutes.

Add the cabbage, celery, beef broth and drained haricot beans. Bring to the boil and season well to taste with salt and pepper. Lower the heat and cover the pan. Simmer gently for 2¾ hours or until the beans are tender.

Add all the remaining ingredients and continue to simmer for a further 15 to 20 minutes or until the macaroni is just tender. Serve very hot and accompany with the Parmesan cheese.

Minestrone

Zuppa di pomodori   Tomato soup

12 ripe tomatoes, skinned
1 garlic clove, chopped
2 tablespoons (2½T) olive oil
2 level tablespoons (2½T)
tomato concentrate
¾ pint (2 cups) chicken stock
3 level tablespoons (3¾T) finely
chopped parsley
1 level teaspoon sugar
salt and pepper to taste
2 level tablespoons (2½T)
cornflour (cornstarch)
4 tablespoons (5T) cold water
serves 4–6

Chop the tomatoes and put them into a saucepan with the garlic, oil, tomato concentrate and stock. Bring to the boil, lower the heat and cover the pan. Simmer gently for 15 minutes. Stir in the parsley, sugar and salt and pepper to taste.

Mix the cornflour (cornstarch) to a smooth cream with the cold water. Add an equal quantity of hot soup then stir well and return to the saucepan. Cook, stirring, until the soup comes to the boil and thickens. Simmer for 5 minutes, adjust the seasoning to taste then serve straight away.

note: if fresh basil is available, chop a few of the leaves and sprinkle them over each portion of soup.

Pea soup

Minestra di fagioli — Haricot bean soup

2 tablespoons (2½T) olive oil
1–2 garlic cloves, chopped
6 oz. (¾ cup) haricot beans,
soaked overnight
1 medium onion, grated
1 medium carrot, grated
2½ pints (6¼ cups) chicken stock
or broth
salt and pepper to taste
4 level tablespoons (5T)
chopped parsley
serves 4–6

A speciality from the province of Tuscany.

Put the oil and garlic into a saucepan and heat until hot. Add the drained beans, onion, carrot, half the stock or broth and salt and pepper to taste. Bring to the boil, lower the heat and cover the pan. Simmer gently until the beans are tender: 2½ to 3 hours.
Either rub the soup through a sieve or blend until smooth in an electric blender. Return to a clean saucepan, add the rest of the stock or broth and heat slowly until hot, stirring.
Adjust the seasoning to taste, stir in the parsley, then serve straight away.

Zuppa di piselli — Pea soup

1 small onion, chopped
2 medium celery stalks, chopped
1 level dessertspoon (1T) each,
melted butter and olive oil
2 lb. fresh peas (approximately
2 cups when shelled)
1 small ham bone
¾ pint (2 cups) chicken stock
or water
1 level tablespoon (1¼T)
cornflour (cornstarch)
½ pint (1¼ cups) cold milk
salt and pepper to taste

serves 4

A soup which demands fresh peas; canned or frozen ones will not do at all.

Fry the onion and celery very gently in the butter and oil until soft but not brown. Add the peas and cook gently, stirring frequently, for a further 5 minutes.
Add the ham bone and stock or water. Bring to the boil, lower the heat and cover the pan. Simmer gently, stirring occasionally, until the peas are very soft; 30 to 40 minutes.
Remove the ham bone, then either rub the soup through a sieve or blend until smooth in an electric blender. Return to a clean saucepan.
Mix the cornflour to a smooth liquid with the cold milk. Add to the soup. Cook, stirring continuously, until the soup comes to the boil and thickens. Simmer for 5 minutes. Season to taste with salt and pepper and serve straight away.

Zuppa di funghi   Mushroom soup

2 oz. (¼ cup) butter
1–2 garlic cloves, chopped
12 oz. (3¾ cups)
sliced mushrooms
3 level tablespoons (3¾T) flour
¾ pint (2 cups) warm chicken
stock or broth
¾ pint (2 cups) milk
salt and pepper to taste
½ breakfast cup (½ cup)
chopped parsley
grated nutmeg
serves 4–6

Heat the butter in a saucepan. Add the garlic and mushrooms and fry gently for 5 minutes, turning all the time.
Stir in the flour, then gradually blend in the warm stock or broth, followed by the milk. Bring to the boil, stirring. Simmer for 5 minutes, then season to taste with salt and pepper and stir in the parsley.
Serve straight away and sprinkle the top of each with nutmeg.

Zuppa di spinaci   Spinach soup

2 oz. (¼ cup) butter
1 garlic clove, chopped
2 level tablespoons (2½T) flour
½ pint (1¼ cups) spinach purée
1½ pints (3¾ cups) chicken stock
or water
¼ pint (⅝ cup) single cream
(coffee cream)
salt and pepper to taste
serves 4–6

Spinach is a well-loved vegetable in Italy and one of its favourite uses is in this delicious soup, which comes from the North East.

Melt the butter in a saucepan. Add the garlic and fry gently for 5 minutes.
Stir in the flour. Gradually blend in the spinach purée, stock or water and the cream.
Cook, stirring continuously, until the soup comes to the boil and thickens. Simmer for 10 minutes then serve straight away.

Zuppa di lentecchie   Lentil soup

½ lb. (1 cup) lentils,
soaked overnight
1 medium onion, chopped
2 medium celery
stalks, chopped
2 tablespoons (2½T) olive oil
2 level tablespoons (2½T)
tomato concentrate
1 to 2 garlic cloves,
finely chopped
2 pints (5 cups) chicken stock
or water
salt and pepper to taste
2 level tablespoons (2½T)
chopped parsley
2 oz. (approximately ½ cup)
pastini (small pasta in the
shape of stars, alphabets,
rice etc.)
grilled bacon rashers, cut into
strips (optional)
serves 4

Drain the lentils. Fry the onion and celery in the oil until soft but not brown.
Add the lentils, tomato concentrate, garlic, stock or water and salt and pepper to taste. Bring to the boil, lower the heat and cover the pan. Simmer gently, stirring occasionally, for approximately 1 hour or until lentils are soft.
Add the parsley and the pastini and continue to simmer for a further 10 minutes. Serve very hot, adding grilled bacon rashers (strips) if liked.

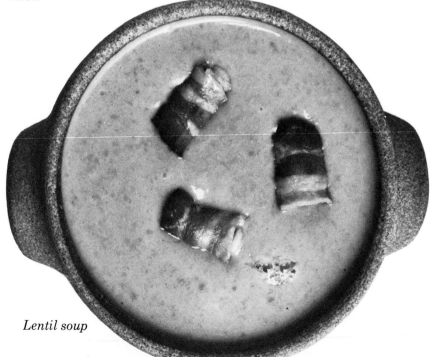

Lentil soup

Zuppa di patate Potato soup

1 large onion, chopped
2 tablespoons (2½T) olive oil
4 large potatoes
1 small ham bone
2 pints (5 cups) chicken stock
   or broth
salt and pepper to taste
3 tablespoons (3¾T) single
   (coffee) cream
grated nutmeg
serves 4

A quickly and easily-made soup for winter eating.

Fry the onion gently in the oil until soft but not brown.
Coarsely grate the potatoes and add to the pan with the ham bone,
stock or broth and salt and pepper to taste. Bring to the boil, cover
the pan and simmer slowly for about 20 minutes.
Stir in the cream and sprinkle the top of each portion very lightly
with nutmeg.

Potato soup

Zuppa di pesce Fish soup

2 tablespoons (2½T) olive oil
2 garlic cloves, chopped
8 large tomatoes, skinned and chopped
4 level tablespoons (5T) finely chopped parsley
2 level tablespoons (2½T) tomato concentrate
1 small onion, chopped
1 celery stalk, finely chopped
¼ pint (⅝ cup) dry white wine
¼ pint (⅝ cup) water
1 level teaspoon sugar
salt and pepper to taste
1 lb. smoked cod fillet
½ lb. firm white fish fillet
1 teacup (¾ cup) peeled prawns, shrimp or pieces of lobster or crab
4–6 anchovy fillets, chopped
serves 4

Quite obviously, exact replicas of the superb fish soups (which, in fact, are more like stews) found along the coastlines of Italy cannot be made because the exotic fish common to those waters are hard to find elsewhere. Nevertheless, with a few modifications, highly successful substitutes are possible and below are two fish soup recipes which we have always enjoyed and taken pleasure in making.

Heat the oil in a saucepan. Add garlic and fry gently for 5 minutes. Stir in the tomatoes, parsley, tomato concentrate, onion, celery, wine, water, sugar and salt and pepper to taste. (Not too much salt, though, as the smoked fish and anchovies contribute some of their own.) Bring to the boil and cover. Lower the heat and simmer for 15 minutes.
Meanwhile, skin the fish and cut the flesh into large chunks. Add to the soup and cook for 5 minutes.
Add the prawns etc. and anchovies and cook for a further 3 minutes. Serve in large plates and accompany with crusty French bread.

Zuppa di cozze Mussel soup

¼ pint (⅝ cup) olive oil
4 garlic cloves, halved
1 small onion, chopped
4 level tablespoons (5T) finely chopped parsley
¼ pint (⅝ cup) dry white wine
¼ pint (⅝ cup) water
2 level tablespoons (2½T) tomato concentrate
6 large tomatoes, skinned and chopped
1 medium celery stalk, chopped
salt and pepper to taste
4 pints (10 cups) mussels
serves 4

A feast for mussel lovers.

Heat the oil in a large frying pan. Add the garlic and onion and fry gently until pale gold.
Stir in the parsley, wine, water, tomato concentrate, tomatoes, celery and salt and pepper to taste. Cook slowly, uncovered, until the liquid is reduced by about a third.
Meanwhile, prepare the mussels. Cut off the beards with kitchen scissors. Transfer the mussels to a colander and wash under cold running water, shaking the colander all the time to prevent the mussels from opening.
Add the mussels to the hot tomato soup and cook fairly briskly for approximately 10 minutes or until all the mussels have opened. Serve in deep plates and accompany with freshly made toast.

Brodo di manzo Beef broth

2 lb. boiling beef
1 lb. soup bones
4 pints (10 cups) water
2 large onions
2 medium carrots
3 medium celery stalks, each broken into 4
1 small turnip
½ breakfast cup (¼ cup) parsley
3 to 4 level teaspoons salt

serves 8–10

This is a relatively uncomplicated beef broth usually served with the same pastini as given in the recipe for zuppa di lentecchie. It is a clear, light soup and may be found in most parts of Italy.

Put the beef (in one piece), the bones, water, onions, carrots, celery stalks, turnip and parsley into a large saucepan. Add salt. Bring to the boil then remove the scum as it rises to the surface. Lower the heat, cover the pan and simmer gently for 4 hours with the heat as low as possible.
Strain into a clean bowl and refrigerate when cold.
Before serving, remove the hard layer of fat from the top and re-heat as much soup as is required. Add pastini to each serving.

Brodo misto Beef and chicken broth

serves 8–10

This is a combination of chicken and beef broth which, like the previous recipe, forms the basis of a number of soups.
To make it, simply follow the recipe for brodo di manzo but use 1 lb. boiling fowl or chicken giblets instead of the soup bones.

Fish soup

Brodo con farfallo
Beef broth with farfalle pasta

Make the beef stock exactly as directed in the recipe for brodo di manzo (page 30), then add bow-shaped pasta (farfalle) to each serving.

Zuppa pavese
Pavese soup

A nourishing soup meal which makes an excellent lunch or supper dish.
Prepare brodo di manzo or brodo misto as directed.
For 4 servings, fry 4 slices of bread in olive oil until crisp and golden on both sides.
Transfer to 4 individual soup bowls and top each with a lightly poached egg.
Fill the bowls with hot broth, sprinkle with grated Parmesan cheese and serve straight away.

Stracciatella
Egg-laced broth

1–1¼ pints (2½–3 cups) brodo di manzo or brodo misto
2 eggs
1 level tablespoon (1¼T) semolina (cream of wheat)
3 level tablespoons (3¾T) grated Parmesan cheese

serves 4

A popular soup all over Italy, although stracciatella—or egg drop soup—comes from Rome.

Put the brodo di manzo or brodo misto on to heat.
Meanwhile, fork-beat the eggs with the semolina (cream of wheat), grated Parmesan cheese and ½ a cup of the hot broth.
Pour back into the hot soup and bring just up to the boil, whisking continuously. As the egg cooks, it will separate out into shreds and give the soup its characteristic—ragged—appearance.

Brodo di manzo e prosciutto
Beef and ham broth

Make exactly as brodo di manzo, adding 1 large ham bone instead of the soup bones. Include also 2 tablespoons (2½T) tomato concentrate. Serve each portion with freshly cooked rice instead of pastini and sprinkle with grated Parmesan cheese.

Pasta in brodo
Tomato and beef broth with macaroni

Make up brodo di manzo as directed but include 2 level tablespoons (2½T) tomato concentrate and 4 large skinned and chopped tomatoes. Serve each portion with freshly cooked elbow macaroni and a little skinned and chopped fresh tomato. Accompany with grated Parmesan cheese.

Zuppa crema di pollo
Cream of chicken soup

2 level tablespoons (2½T) cornflour (cornstarch)
1 pint (2½ cups) cold brodo misto
salt and pepper to taste
½ breakfast cup (½ cup) cooked chicken, cut into strips
¼ pint (⅝ cup) double (heavy) cream
2 egg yolks
grated nutmeg

serves 4–5

A handsome, creamy soup for elegant eating.

Mix the cornflour (cornstarch) to a smooth liquid with a little brodo misto. Add the rest of the brodo misto and cook, stirring continuously, until the soup comes to the boil and thickens.
Season to taste with salt and pepper then add the chicken.
Simmer for 7 minutes.
Beat the cream and egg yolks well together. Pour into the soup and re-heat gently without boiling. Serve each portion lightly sprinkled with nutmeg.

Minestrone Milanese

Pizza
Pasta
Rice
and Gnocchi

These days, **pizza** is so well known that it requires no description, except to say that it should be eaten while still warm and fragrantly fresh. Probably **pasta** requires no description either, for in every big city, supermarket shelves are laden with boxes of macaroni, noodles, spaghetti, lasagne and cannelloni—to name but a few— and cookery books and magazines are equally laden with recipes on how to use them. All we would ask you is to try, just once, the following recipe for pasta. It is good— and when turned into noodles and served with melted butter and grated Parmesan cheese, superb! It needs time, as you will see, but—Rome wasn't built in a day either!

Risotto is almost as well known as pizza and pasta, but outside Italy it rarely tastes or looks authentic and one is all too often confronted with a kind of nondescript pilaff, which is supposed to be risotto but bears little or no resemblance to it whatsoever! A pity. The real thing is so much better and very easy to make, if one is prepared to use the right ingredients. It needs Italian rice above all else or, if this is completely impossible to find, old-fashioned round grain pudding rice. Long grain rice, good though it is, fails with risotto and should be avoided.

Gnocchi can be made from semolina, polenta or potatoes and is a deliciously satisfying dish which deserves to be better known and cooked more frequently than it is. The following recipes for it have been made over and over again with success. The nicest, in our view, is the semolina gnocchi, tastefully flavoured with Parmesan cheese and served, golden brown and sizzling, straight from the oven. With creamy spinach purée and fried or baked tomatoes, it makes a luxurious meal at little cost and is just right for a mid-week lunch or supper dish.

Less difficult to prepare than one would imagine, pasta is a great therapeutic occupation, for it is both fun to make and immensely satisfying. But it requires space, patience and time and if none of these is available, then one is well advised to settle for the packet pastas which are good and in abundant variety.

The varied forms of raw pasta

Pasta alla casalinga   Home made pasta

8 oz. (1½ cups) plain (all purpose) flour
1 level teaspoon salt
1 egg
1 dessertspoon (1T) olive oil
4 tablespoons (5T) hot water

Sift the flour and salt into a bowl and make a well in the centre. Break in the egg, then add the oil and water. Work to a dough with the fingertips.

Turn out on to a floured surface and knead until the dough no longer sticks to the fingers—about 10 to 15 minutes, which is the lengthiest part of the whole operation. Divide the dough into 2 equal-sized pieces.

Cover a working surface with a brightly patterned table cloth or tea towel and flour heavily. Stand one portion of the dough on top. Roll out as thinly as possible then stretch and pull gently with the fingers until the dough is so thin that the pattern from the cloth shows through. The dough is very elastic and therefore stretches fairly easily.

Roll up the piece of dough loosely then cut it into slices, about ¼-inch in thickness. Open out each slice (one noodle) and drape over the back of a chair, first covered with a tea towel.

Repeat with second piece of dough and leave the noodles to dry out for about ½ an hour.

Cook in plenty of boiling salted water for 5 to 7 minutes.

Drain and use as required.

Spaghetti

note: home made pasta takes less time to cook than packet varieties.

Cooking packet pasta

Cooking spaghetti as it is cooked in Italy is an art, but fortunately an art readily mastered if one obeys the basic rules.

First and foremost, pasta must always be al dente; soft without being soggy, and chewy without being hard. Thus cooking time must be watched carefully and between 10 and 12 minutes should be quite long enough for large pasta such as spaghetti and macaroni, while no longer than 5 to 7 minutes should be allowed for small pasta (pastini).

The amount of pasta per person depends on appetite and the kind of meal. Quite obviously, less pasta is needed for a meal starter than for a main course and the amount, therefore, can vary from 2 oz. per person to 4 oz. ($\frac{1}{2}$ to 1 cup).

All pasta should be cooked in plenty of boiling salted water—about $\frac{3}{4}$ pint (2 cups) to each oz. ($\frac{1}{4}$ cup) pasta—drained thoroughly, transferred to a warm dish and served immediately.

note: a little oil added to the cooking water helps to keep the pasta separate.

Ingredients for home made pasta
Cutting macaroni with a rotary
blade cutter

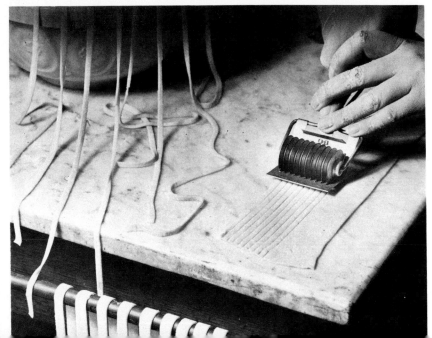

Spaghetti al burro Spaghetti with butter

Cook the spaghetti following the directions for cooking packet pasta.
To make eating easier, it may be broken up first, but strictly
speaking, the spaghetti should be left whole and cooked whole.
To do this, hold one end of the spaghetti strands in the hand and
stand the other end in the saucepan of boiling water. As the spaghetti
softens, it will curl round in the pan and may then be pushed
downwards gradually until it is completely covered with the water.
After cooking, drain thoroughly, put into a large warm dish
containing plenty of butter or olive oil and toss gently with two forks
until each spaghetti strand is coated. Serve straight away with
grated Parmesan cheese.

to vary: cook any different pasta shapes as above, and toss with
butter.
Garnish with fried onions and serve with grated Parmesan cheese.

Spaghetti with butter

Spaghetti alla Bolognese

Spaghetti Bolognese

2 tablespoons (2½T) olive oil
1 medium onion, finely chopped
2 garlic cloves, finely chopped
3 rashers unsmoked bacon (bacon strips)
1 medium celery stalk, finely chopped
1 medium carrot, grated
4 oz. (1¼ cups) sliced mushrooms
8 oz. raw minced (ground) beef
4 level tablespoons (5T) tomato concentrate
1 wine glass dry white or red wine
4 medium tomatoes, skinned and chopped
½ pint (1¼ cups) beef stock
2 level teaspoons brown sugar
pinch of ground nutmeg
freshly cooked spaghetti (see page 37)
grated Parmesan cheese
serves 4

Perhaps the best known and best loved of all the pasta dishes.

Heat the oil in a saucepan. Add the onion, garlic, chopped bacon, celery, carrot and mushrooms. Fry slowly for 7 minutes.
Add the beef and fry for a further 5 minutes, breaking it up with a fork all the time. Add all the remaining ingredients and bring to the boil, stirring. Lower the heat, cover the pan and simmer very gently for 45 minutes, stirring occasionally.
Add to the well-drained spaghetti and toss thoroughly.
Serve with grated Parmesan cheese.

Spaghetti bolognese

Tagliatelle alla Bolognese

Tagliatelle Bolognese

Make exactly as spaghetti Bolognese but use flat ribbon noodles (known as tagliatelle or fettuccine) instead of the spaghetti.

Spaghetti alla carbonara

Spaghetti with ham and eggs

spaghetti (see page 37)
8 bacon rashers (strips)
a little olive oil
2 eggs
2 tablespoons (2½T) single (coffee) cream
grated Parmesan cheese

This simple but delicious combination comes from Rome and is equally good as a starter or as a main course.

Cook the spaghetti as directed. Five minutes before it is ready, chop the bacon rashers (strips) into small pieces and fry gently in a little olive oil for 3 minutes. Beat 2 eggs with 2 tablespoons (2½T) single (coffee) cream. Drain the spaghetti thoroughly and transfer to a warm dish. Add the fried bacon (and any left-over oil or fat from pan), the egg mixture and 2 or 3 level tablespoons (2½–3¾T) grated Parmesan cheese. Toss with two forks until the eggs thicken and scramble with the heat from the pasta. Accompany with extra Parmesan cheese.

serves 4

Spaghetti alla matriciana
Spaghetti with salt pork and tomato

1 tablespoon (1¼T) bacon dripping
1 medium onion, chopped
4 bacon rashers (strips), or equivalent weight of salt pork, cut into thin strips
8 large tomatoes, skinned and chopped
salt and pepper to taste
freshly cooked spaghetti
clove of garlic
1 tablespoon (1¼T) olive oil
grated Pecorino or Parmesan cheese

serves 4

A speciality from the Abruzzo e Molise region, which is noted for its excellent but unsophisticated cuisine.

Heat the dripping in a saucepan. Add the onion and bacon rashers and fry gently for 5 minutes. Add the tomatoes and salt and pepper to taste, then simmer for 5 minutes.

Drain the spaghetti thoroughly and put into a warm serving dish, rubbed first with a cut clove of garlic.

Add the olive oil and toss the spaghetti thoroughly. Pour the sauce on top and accompany with grated Pecorino cheese (if available) or grated Parmesan.

Lasagne

Spaghetti alla marinara
Spaghetti with fresh tomato and basil sauce

2 tablespoons (2½T) olive oil
2–4 garlic cloves, chopped
8 large tomatoes, skinned and chopped
6–8 anchovy fillets, chopped (optional)
2 level teaspoons mint, finely chopped
or 1 level tablespoon (1¼T) parsley, chopped
or 1 level tablespoon (1¼T) fresh basil, chopped
salt and pepper to taste
freshly cooked spaghetti (see page 37)
butter
grated Parmesan cheese

A typically Neapolitan dish, marinara meaning 'sailor-style'.

Make a sauce by heating the olive oil with the chopped garlic cloves. Add the tomatoes and chopped anchovy fillets, if liked. Cook for 5 minutes then add the herbs and season well to taste with salt and pepper. Pour on top of freshly cooked spaghetti, first tossed with butter.
Accompany with grated Parmesan cheese.

Spaghetti al tonno
Spaghetti with tuna

1 oz. (2T) butter
1 tablespoon (1¼T) olive oil
1 can (7 oz.) tuna
¼ pint (⅝ cup) chicken stock
2 level tablespoons (2½T) chopped parsley
salt and pepper to taste
freshly cooked spaghetti

Heat the butter and oil in a saucepan. Break up the tuna and add, with its oil, to the saucepan. Cook gently for 3 minutes.
Add the stock and simmer for a further 5 minutes. Add the parsley and salt and pepper to taste.
Drain the spaghetti thoroughly and put into a warm dish.
Add the tuna sauce, toss well and serve straight away.

Spaghetti Napoletana
Spaghetti Neapolitan

10 very ripe tomatoes, skinned and chopped
1 oz. (2T) butter
1 tablespoon (1¼T) olive oil
1 medium celery stalk, chopped
1 small onion, chopped
2 garlic cloves, chopped
1 level teaspoon sugar
¼ pint (⅝ cup) water
salt and pepper to taste
1 level teaspoon dried basil (or use double the amount of fresh chopped basil if available)
2 level tablespoons (2½T) chopped parsley
freshly cooked spaghetti
grated Parmesan cheese

Put the tomatoes into a pan with the butter, oil, celery, onion, garlic, sugar, water and salt and pepper to taste. Bring to the boil, stirring, then lower the heat and simmer the sauce, uncovered, for 15 minutes. Add the basil and parsley and continue to simmer for a further 20 to 30 minutes until the sauce is thick and purée-like. Drain the spaghetti thoroughly and put into a warm dish. Add the sauce, toss well and accompany with grated Parmesan cheese.

Spaghetti all'olio e aglio
Spaghetti with garlic sauce

freshly cooked spaghetti
5 tablespoons (6¼T) olive oil
4–6 garlic cloves, finely chopped
2 heaped tablespoons (2¾T) parsley, finely chopped
½ level teaspoon dried basil
salt and pepper to taste

Bliss for garlic lovers but possibly a bit overwhelming for those who like milder, gentler food with less aftertaste!

5 minutes before the spaghetti is cooked, heat the olive oil with the garlic cloves. Keep the heat low to avoid frying the garlic. Add the parsley and basil. Drain the spaghetti thoroughly and transfer to a warm dish. Add the oil mixture, season with salt and freshly ground pepper and toss gently. Serve straight away.

Maccheroni al gratin   Macaroni with cheese

8 oz. (2 cups) elbow macaroni
2 oz. (¼ cup) butter
3 level tablespoons (3¾T) flour
¾ pint (2 cups) milk and
macaroni water mixed in
equal proportions
4 oz. (1 cup) grated
Parmesan cheese
salt and pepper to taste
1 oz. (2T) extra butter

serves 4–6

Preheat the oven to moderate (350°F, or Mark 4).
Cook the macaroni in boiling salted water as directed for spaghetti (see page 37). Drain and reserve 1½ gills (1 cup) macaroni water.
Melt the butter in a saucepan. Stir in the flour and cook for 2 minutes without browning. Gradually blend in the macaroni water followed by the milk. Cook, stirring, until the sauce comes to the boil and thickens. Simmer for 2 minutes. Stir in ¾ of the cheese then season well to taste with salt and pepper.
Transfer to a buttered heatproof dish. Sprinkle the rest of the cheese on top then dot with flakes of butter. Reheat in the centre of the oven for 30 minutes.

Maccheroni alla pizzaiola   Macaroni with tomato, garlic and herbs

12 medium sized ripe tomatoes,
skinned and chopped
2 tablespoons (2½T) olive oil
2 garlic cloves, chopped
1 heaped tablespoon (1½T)
parsley, coarsely chopped
½ level teaspoon oregano
1 level teaspoon
granulated sugar
salt and pepper to taste
freshly cooked macaroni
grated Parmesan or
Pecorino cheese

serves 4

Put the tomatoes into a saucepan with the oil, garlic, parsley, oregano, sugar and salt and pepper to taste. Bring to the boil, lower the heat and simmer, uncovered, for 15 minutes.
Drain the macaroni thoroughly and transfer to a warm dish.
Add the tomato sauce and toss.
Accompany with grated Parmesan cheese or Pecorino cheese.

Macaroni with cheese and bacon pieces

*Meat balls and tomato sauce
with spaghetti (below)*

Risotto (right)

Pizza Neapolitan (far right)

*Tagliatelle with liver sauce (below
far right)*

45

Maccheroni con piselli
Macaroni with peas

2 tablespoons (2½T) olive oil
4 oz. (1 cup) cubed ham, very finely chopped
1 small onion, chopped
1 garlic clove, chopped
2 medium celery stalks, chopped
6 large tomatoes, skinned and chopped
½ pint (1¼ cups) chicken stock
2 level tablespoons (2½T) tomato concentrate
1 heaped tablespoon (1½T) parsley, chopped
6 oz. (1 cup) fresh peas, shelled
salt and pepper to taste
freshly cooked macaroni (see page 37)
fresh basil or mint

serves 4

Heat the oil in a saucepan. Add the ham, onion, garlic and celery. Fry gently for 7 minutes. Add the tomatoes, stock, tomato concentrate, parsley, peas and salt and pepper to taste. Bring to the boil, lower the heat and simmer gently for 30 minutes.
Drain the macaroni and transfer to a warm dish. Add the sauce and toss thoroughly.
Serve straight away and dust each portion with a little finely chopped fresh basil or mint.

Lasagne
Lasagne

6 oz. lasagne
1 recipe Bolognese sauce (see page 39)
1 recipe cheese sauce (see page 43)
nutmeg
grated Parmesan cheese
butter

serves 4

Cook the leaves of lasagne in plenty of boiling salted water for 10 to 15 minutes. Drain thoroughly, then stand each piece on paper towelling to absorb surplus moisture. Butter a fairly deep heatproof dish well. Cover the base with the Bolognese sauce. Add a layer of cheese sauce to which a dash of ground nutmeg has been added. Top with lasagne leaves.
Repeat, finishing with a layer of cheese sauce topped with a little Bolognese sauce. Sprinkle thickly with Parmesan cheese then dot with flakes of butter. Re-heat for 30 minutes in the centre of a moderate oven (350°F, Mark 4).
Serve straight away with a green salad.

Lasagne verdi
Lasagne with spinach

Make exactly as above but use lasagne verdi which, during manufacture, is coloured green through the addition of spinach.

Tagliatelle con fegatini di pollo
Tagliatelle with liver sauce

8 oz. (1 cup) chicken livers
2 level tablespoons (2½T) flour
1 oz. (2T) butter
1 tablespoon (1¼T) olive oil
1 small onion, finely chopped
1 small garlic clove, chopped
4 oz. (1¼ cups) mushrooms, sliced
¼ pint (⅝ cup) chicken stock
¼ pint (⅝ cup) dry white wine
salt and pepper to taste
freshly cooked tagliatelle (see page 37)

A substantial dish which may be made with spaghetti or macaroni as well as with tagliatelle.

Cut the livers into small pieces and coat with flour.
Heat the butter and oil in a saucepan. Add the onion and garlic and fry gently until pale gold. Add the liver and mushrooms. Fry more briskly for 3 to 4 minutes, stirring all the time.
Add the stock and wine, then season well to taste with salt and pepper. Bring to the boil, stirring, then lower the heat and cover the pan. Simmer gently for 15 minutes.
Transfer the tagliatelle to a warm dish. Add the sauce, toss well and serve straight away.

Tagliatelle alle acciughe
Tagliatelle with anchovy sauce

1 tablespoon (1¼T) olive oil
2 oz. (¼ cup) butter
2 garlic cloves, finely chopped
1 small can anchovy fillets
½ teacup (⅜ cup) parsley,
finely chopped
½ level teaspoon oregano
pepper to taste
freshly cooked tagliatelle (see
page 37)

A potent brew which oils and flavours the pasta in hearty fashion.

Heat the oil and butter in a saucepan. Add the garlic and heat very slowly for 5 minutes.
Open the anchovies and drain the oil into the saucepan. Chop the anchovies and add to the pan with parsley and oregano. Heat through for 5 minutes then season to taste with freshly milled pepper. Drain the tagliatelle and transfer to a warm dish. Add the anchovy mixture and toss well. Serve straight away.

47

nnelloni with cheese sauce

Cannelloni Cannelloni

8 oz. cannelloni
1 breakfast cup (1 cup) cubes of
stewed beef
1½ oz. (¾ cup) fresh white
breadcrumbs
2 oz. (½ cup) grated
Parmesan cheese
1 beaten egg
¼ level teaspoon ground nutmeg
a little gravy from the
stewed beef
salt and pepper to taste
1 oz. (2T) butter
¼ pint (⅝ cup) chicken stock
serves 4

Cook the cannelloni in boiling salted water for 8 to 10 minutes.
Drain thoroughly. When cool enough to handle, split each one
lengthwise and open out.
To make the stuffing, mince the stewed beef finely and combine with
the breadcrumbs, half the cheese, egg and nutmeg. Bind with a little
gravy then season well to taste with salt and pepper.
Put equal amounts of the stuffing on to each cannelloni, then roll up
like fat sausages. Place side by side in a shallow buttered heatproof
dish. Dot with flakes of butter then sprinkle with the rest of the
cheese. Pour the stock into the dish then re-heat in the centre of a
moderate oven (350°F, Mark 4) for 25 to 30 minutes.

Home made Cannelloni

Prepare the dough as directed for basic pasta (see page 36). Roll out
thinly and cut into squares measuring 3 × 4 inches. Cook in plenty of
boiling salted water, to which 1 or 2 teaspoons of oil have been
added, for about 5 minutes. Drain thoroughly, then fill and roll
as above.

Artichoke omelette

Ravioli verdi   Ravioli with spinach

dough (see page 36)
filling
3 oz. (⅜ cup) spinach purée
2 oz. (¼ cup) Italian Ricotta
cheese or curd cheese
1 oz. (¼ cup) grated
Parmesan cheese
½ a beaten egg
1½ level dessertspoons
(1¼ T) flour
1 teaspoon melted butter
salt, pepper and ground nutmeg
to taste

serves 4

Divide the dough into 2 equal-sized portions and roll both out very
thinly, making one slightly larger than the other.
To make the filling, combine all the ingredients well together and
beat until smooth.
Stand the smaller piece of rolled dough on to a floured surface.
Brush with water and cover with small heaps of filling, leaving
plenty of space round each.
Cover with the second piece of dough, allowing it to lie loosely over
the first piece. Stamp out the ravioli with a fluted biscuit cutter,
cutting round the dough and avoiding the filling.
Place in a single layer, on a floured board or plate, dust with flour
and cover with a tea towel. Leave in a cool place until required.
To cook, drop gently into plenty of boiling salted water and simmer
for about 5 minutes or until the ravioli float to the top. Lift out of the
saucepan with a perforated spoon and serve with plenty of butter
and grated Parmesan cheese.

a

b

Preparing ravioli
(a) Filling ravioli cases
(b) Stamping out the ravioli with
a fluted biscuit cutter

Ravioli Meat ravioli

**4 oz. (½ cup) finely minced
(ground) stewed beef
½ oz. (¼ cup) fresh
white breadcrumbs
¼ level teaspoon dried thyme
salt and pepper to taste**
serves 4

Make exactly as the spinach/cheese ravioli given in the previous
recipe, but fill with a mixture of beef, breadcrumbs and seasoning.

Raviolo con Sugo di
Pomodoro Meat ravioli with tomato sauce.

Prepare the ravioli as above.
Heat the ravioli in any of the tomato sauces suggested for pasta.
Sprinkle with grated Parmesan cheese and serve hot.

Meat ravioli

Risotto in cagnon — Risotto

1 oz. (2T) butter
2 teaspoons olive oil
1 small onion, finely chopped
12 oz. (2 cups) Italian rice
1 wine glass dry white wine
2 pints (5 cups) hot water
salt and pepper to taste
1 extra oz. (2T) butter
4 level tablespoons (5T)
Parmesan cheese

Risotto is a classic dish of the North—the most famous version being risotto Milanese—and, when properly cooked, is one of the delights of Italian cuisine. Risotto is almost always eaten as a dish by itself and rarely accompanies anything other than osso buco (see page 77, the equally well-known and robust veal stew from Milan.

Heat the butter and oil in a large saucepan. Add the onion and fry very gently, covered, for 5 minutes or until the onion is soft but still white.

Add the rice and cook gently for 3 minutes, turning all the time until each rice grain is coated with butter and oil. Add the wine and cook over a moderate heat until it evaporates. Blend in the stock, gradually adding more as each amount becomes absorbed by the rice. Stir frequently with a fork and allow 20 to 30 minutes cooking time, when the rice should be creamy but still firm.

Using a fork, stir in extra butter and the Parmesan cheese and serve straight away. Pass extra butter and Parmesan cheese separately.

Risotto alla Milanese — Risotto Milanese

Follow the recipe for plain risotto but after frying the onion and before adding the rice, add 1 oz. raw beef marrow taken from a marrow bone. Use chicken stock instead of water and when the rice has absorbed all the liquid, stir in a large pinch of powdered saffron with the extra butter and Parmesan cheese.

Risotto con prosciutto — Ham risotto

Another version of risotto which comes from Verona in the region of Venice.

Make a plain risotto as directed but stir in 4 oz. (1 cup) cubed ham with the extra butter and Parmesan cheese.

Risotto alla finanziera — Risotto with sweetbreads

Make a plain risotto as directed.

While it is cooking, fry 1 small chopped onion and 1 breakfast cup (1 cup) chicken livers in 2 oz. (¼ cup) butter for 10 minutes.

Add ½ wine glass Marsala and cook a little more briskly until Marsala evaporates.

Stir the livers etc. into the cooked risotto, just before the extra butter and Parmesan cheese.

serves 4

Risotto alla sbirraglia — Chicken risotto

Make a plain risotto as directed but use chicken stock instead of water.

When the rice is half cooked, add 1 breakfast cup (1 cup) freshly boiled diced chicken.

Stir in extra butter and Parmesan cheese at the end and serve straight away.

serves 4

Risotto di frutta di mare   Seafood risotto

Make exactly as risotto alla Milanese but omit the beef marrow.
5 minutes before the risotto has finished cooking, fry 8 oz. (2 cups) shelled seafood (lobster, shrimp or scampi) in a little butter for 2 or 3 minutes. Add half a wine glass Marsala and cook briskly until the Marsala evaporates. Add to the risotto just before stirring in extra butter and Parmesan cheese.

note: the flavour of this risotto is improved if made with half water and half fish stock.
To make a reasonable fish stock, simmer for approximately 30 minutes, 1 lb. fish trimmings, 1 sliced onion, 1 celery stalk, 1 carrot, $\frac{1}{2}$ bay leaf, and 2 level teaspoons salt in 1 pint ($2\frac{1}{2}$ cups) water. Strain and use as required.

serves 4

Risotto di peoci   Risotto with mussels

Another speciality from Venice.

Prepare a plain risotto as directed.
Meanwhile wash and scrub 4 pints (10 cups) mussels. Heat 4 tablespoons (5T) olive oil and 1 oz. (2T) butter in a large saucepan. Add 2 finely chopped garlic cloves and 2 heaped tablespoons chopped parsley.
Add the mussels and leave over a medium heat until they open. When cool enough to handle, take the mussels out of their shells and add to the risotto with mussel liquor, followed by extra butter and Parmesan cheese.

serves 4

Risotto with mussels

Risotto con agnello Lamb risotto

8 oz. lamb fillet, cut from top
of leg
2 oz. (¼ cup) butter
1 medium onion, finely chopped
4 medium tomatoes, skinned
and chopped
12 oz. (2 cups) Italian rice
1 wine glass dry white wine
2 pints (5 cups) chicken stock
salt and pepper to taste
4 level tablespoons (5T) grated
Parmesan cheese
serves 4

A more unusual risotto from Venice.

Cut the raw lamb fillet into tiny cubes. Heat the butter in a saucepan. Add the onion and fry slowly until pale gold. Add the lamb and fry a little more briskly until the pieces are well sealed and golden. Add the tomatoes and rice and cook for 2 minutes, stirring frequently. Add the wine and cook over a low heat until it evaporates. Blend in the stock gradually, adding more as each amount becomes absorbed by the rice.
Stir frequently with a fork and allow 20 to 30 minutes cooking time, when the rice should be creamy but still firm. Stir in the Parmesan cheese and serve straight away.

Risi e bisi Venetian risotto with green peas

2 rashers streaky bacon
(bacon strips)
2 oz. (¼ cup) butter
1 small onion, finely chopped
12 oz. (2 cups) shelled peas
3 pints (7½ cups) hot chicken
or beef stock
12 oz. (2 cups) Italian rice
2 heaped tablespoons (2¾T)
parsley, finely chopped
salt and pepper to taste
3 oz. (¾ cup) grated
Parmesan cheese
serves 4

Also from Venice comes this rice and green pea risotto-style dish, which is now world famous. It is more liquidy than the standard risotto and therefore is usually eaten with a spoon.

Chop the bacon finely. Heat the butter in a large pan. Add the bacon and onion and fry gently until pale gold.
Add the peas and 4 teacups (3 cups) of the stock. Cover and simmer for 10 minutes. Add the rice, then very gradually blend in the rest of the stock, adding more as each amount becomes absorbed by the rice. Stir frequently with a wooden fork and allow about 20 to 25 minutes cooking time, when the rice should be soft and most of the liquid absorbed.
Stir in the parsley, salt and pepper to taste and the cheese. Serve straight away.

La polenta Polenta

1¼ pints (3 cups) boiling water
2 level teaspoons salt
7 oz. (1 cup) polenta

Polenta is a warm, golden-yellow flour—rather like semolina in appearance—made from maize. It is very much favoured in Northern Italy where it is cooked in water and then eaten with butter and cheese or with tomato or Bolognese sauce. Polenta is traditional, comforting and very typically Italian and makes a satisfying substitute for potatoes, pasta or rice. It is also used to accompany small roast game birds such as pigeons and quails.

Pour the boiling water into a saucepan and add salt. Tip in all the polenta then bring slowly to the boil, stirring continuously. At once lower the heat and simmer very slowly, stirring frequently, for 20 minutes or until the polenta is very thick.
Serve each portion liberally topped with flakes of butter and grated Parmesan cheese or coat with the sauces suggested above and then
serves 4–6 sprinkle with grated cheese.

Chicken breasts with shell pasta,
chicken pilaff and varied raw
pasta

La pizza Napoletana   Pizza Neapolitan

dough base
¼ level teaspoon sugar
¼ pint (⅝ cu) warm water (110°F)
1 level teaspoon dried yeast
8 oz. (1½ cups) plain (all-purpose) flour
1 level teaspoon salt
1 dessertspoon (1T) butter

filling
olive oil
6 medium tomatoes, skinned and sliced
1 garlic clove, chopped
12 anchovy fillets
4 oz. Mozzarella cheese, thinly sliced
6 large black olives, stoned
oregano
pepper
serves 2

To make the dough, dissolve the sugar in the warm water and sprinkle the dried yeast on top. Leave in a warmish place for 10 to 16 minutes or until frothy.

Meanwhile, sift the flour and salt into a bowl and rub in the butter. Mix to a dough with the yeast liquid, adding a little extra flour if the dough is sticky. Knead for a good 10 minutes or until the dough is smooth and elastic, then put into an oiled bowl. Cover with oiled paper and leave to rise until the dough doubles in size.

Turn out on to a floured surface then knead lightly until smooth. Roll out into a ¼-inch thick circle and stand on an oiled baking tray. Brush with olive oil then cover with slices of tomato. Sprinkle with garlic. Top with anchovy fillets, slices of cheese and the olives. Sprinkle with the oregano and pepper then bake near the top of a hot oven (450°F, Mark 8) for 25 to 30 minutes.

Serve while still warm.

Pizza neapolitan

56

Pizza al prosciutto
Ham pizza

Make exactly as pizza alla Neapolitana but use 2 oz. ($\frac{1}{2}$ cup) coarsely chopped ham instead of the anchovies.

Pizza con funghi e olivi
Pizza with mushrooms and olives

Make the dough exactly as given for pizza alla Neapolitana. Cover with 4 skinned and sliced tomatoes, 1 small chopped garlic clove, 4 oz. ($1\frac{1}{4}$ cups) sliced mushrooms (first fried in a little butter) and 12 sliced pimento-stuffed olives.

Pizza al salame
Pizza with salami

Make exactly as pizza alla Neapolitana but omit the anchovy fillets. Use 6 to 8 thin slices of Italian salami instead.

Pizzette
Small pizza

Roll the dough out into 4 equal sized rounds. Stand on an oiled baking tray and cover as directed for any of the other pizza. Bake for 15 to 20 minutes.

Gnocchi alla Romana
Semolina gnocchi

1 pint ($2\frac{1}{2}$ cups) milk
5 oz. ($\frac{3}{4}$ cup) coarse semolina (cream of wheat)
1 level teaspoon salt
shake of pepper
2 oz. ($\frac{1}{4}$ cup) butter
3 oz. ($\frac{3}{4}$ cup) grated Parmesan cheese
$\frac{1}{4}$ level teaspoon ground nutmeg
1 large egg, beaten
1 extra oz. (2T) butter

Pour the milk into a saucepan. Add the semolina, salt, pepper and butter. Stir continuously over a low heat until the mixture comes to the boil and thickens. Continue to simmer until the mixture is very thick; anything from 5 to 7 minutes. Stir frequently to prevent sticking.
Remove from the heat then beat in 2 oz. ($\frac{1}{2}$ cup) cheese, nutmeg and egg. Beat until well mixed then turn out on to a flat dish or tin, spreading the mixture to $\frac{1}{4}$-inch thick. Leave in the cool for several hours or until firm, then cut into $1\frac{1}{2}$-inch squares or rounds with a knife or cutter dipped in cold water.
Butter a shallow heatproof dish well, then fill with layers of the gnocchi squares or rounds and arrange in overlapping circles. Sprinkle with the rest of the cheese then top with flakes of extra butter. Re-heat and brown towards the top of a hot oven (425°F, Mark 7) for 15 minutes.

serves 4

Gnocchi di prosciutto
Ham gnocchi

Make as the previous recipe, but add 4 level tablespoons (5T) very finely chopped ham with the cheese. 1 or 2 level tablespoons ($1\frac{1}{4}$–$2\frac{1}{2}$T) parsley may also be included, as may 1 or 2 level teaspoons very finely grated onion.

serves 4

Gnocchi di polenta
Polenta gnocchi

Make exactly as semolina gnocchi, using polenta instead of semolina.

Gnocchi di patate   Potato gnocchi

1 lb. potatoes (before peeling)
4 oz. (½ cup) plain
(all-purpose) flour
1 teaspoon butter
1 beaten egg
plenty of salt and pepper
to taste
butter
grated Parmesan cheese

serves 4

A substantial form of gnocchi which is suitable either as a starter or as a main course.

Cook the potatoes in boiling salted water until tender. Drain thoroughly. Stand the pan of potatoes on the lowest possible heat and mash finely with a fork or masher. Alternatively—and this is the best method—rub the potatoes through a sieve.
Transfer to a bowl, then work in the flour, butter, beaten egg and salt and pepper to taste. Knead until the mixture is smooth then, with damp hands, shape pieces of the mixture into small balls. Drop into a saucepan of boiling salted water and cook until the gnocchi float to the top. Lift out of the pan with a perforated spoon and transfer to a warm dish. Top with pieces of butter then sprinkle with Parmesan cheese and serve straight away.

Gnocchi con salsa di fegatini   Potato gnocchi with liver sauce

Cook the potato gnocchi as directed then serve with liver sauce, see tagliatelle with liver sauce, page 46

Polenta gnocchi

Eggs

Italian egg dishes are similar to those found anywhere else. Familiarity in this instance is both endearing and surprising when one finds, under a blue Mediterranean sky, the frittata—or omelette—packed with all sorts of fillings, or scrambled eggs with Parmesan cheese or salami, sophisticated baked eggs or the famous egg and spinach combination known as egg Florentine.

Uova alla Fiorentina Eggs Florentine

½ pint (1¼ cups) spinach purée
1 dessertspoon (IT) butter
1 tablespoon (1¼T) double
(heavy) cream
pinch of ground nutmeg
1 oz. (2T) butter
2 level tablespoons (2½T) flour
½ pint (1¼ cups) milk
3 oz. (¾ cup) grated
Parmesan cheese
salt and pepper to taste
4 eggs
1 level tablespoon (1¼T) fine
white breadcrumbs
serves 4

A classic luncheon or supper dish.

Heat the spinach purée with the butter and cream. Remove from the heat and add the nutmeg. Arrange in a buttered heatproof dish and keep warm.

Melt the butter in a pan. Stir in the flour and cook for 2 minutes without browning. Gradually blend in the milk. Cook, stirring continuously until the sauce comes to the boil and thickens. Simmer for 2 minutes. Add 2 oz. (½ cup) cheese and stir until melted. Season to taste with salt and pepper.

Poach the eggs lightly and arrange on top of the spinach. Pour over the sauce, coat with the remaining cheese and crumbs and brown under a hot grill. Serve straight away.

Uova in tazzine Baked eggs

4 level tablespoons (5T) grated
Parmesan cheese
4 level tablespoons (5T) Italian
ham or salami, finely chopped
4 tablespoons (5T) double
(heavy) cream
4 eggs
salt and pepper
1 dessertspoon (1T)
melted butter
serves 4

Preheat the oven to moderate (350°F, Mark 4).
Butter 4 individual heatproof dishes well.
Sprinkle the base of each dish with the cheese and ham or salami, then pour in a tablespoon of cream. Break an egg into each and sprinkle with salt and pepper. Spoon the butter over the tops then stand in a roasting pan containing ½-inch cold water.
Cook in the centre of the oven for approximately 8 minutes or until the whites are set and the yokes still creamy. Serve straight away.

*Scrambled eggs with cheese,
surrounded by (left to right)
bacon rolls, mushrooms, braised
pimentos and tomatoes, croutons,
mussels and kidneys*

Uova strapazzate al formaggio

Scrambled eggs with cheese

1 oz. (2T) butter
4 tablespoons (5T) single (coffee) cream
8 eggs, beaten
salt and pepper to taste
4 level tablespoons (5T) grated Parmesan cheese
1 level teaspoon very finely chopped fresh basil or 2 level teaspoons finely chopped parsley
serves 4

Heat the butter and cream in a saucepan. Add the eggs, salt and pepper to taste and 2 tablespoons ($2\frac{1}{2}$T) of the cheese. Scramble over a low heat until the eggs are just set.
Transfer to a warm dish. Sprinkle with the rest of the cheese and basil or parsley.

Uova strapazzate con salame

Scrambled eggs with salami

Make exactly as scrambled eggs with cheese but include 8 thin slices of Italian salami, cut into thin strips. Add to the pan with the beaten eggs.

Baked eggs

61

Frittata di carciofi   Artichoke omelette

2 canned or fresh
artichoke hearts
1 oz. (2T) butter
3 eggs
3 teaspoons water
salt and pepper to taste
1 level tablespoon (1¼T) grated
Parmesan cheese

serves 1

Cut the artichoke hearts into quarters and fry gently in half the butter while preparing the omelette.
Beat the eggs lightly with water and salt and pepper to taste. Heat the rest of the butter to sizzling point in an 8-inch omelette pan, keeping the heat fairly high. Pour in the egg mixture, then draw the edges towards the centre with a knife, at the same time tilting the pan in all directions so that the uncooked egg flows back to the edges and gets cooked (about 1 minute).
Arrange the artichoke hearts on one half of the omelette, sprinkle with cheese then fold the omelette over. Slide out on to a warm plate and serve straight away.

Frittata Genovese   Spinach omelette

serves 1

Prepare the omelette exactly as directed for frittata al carciofi but fill with 4 or 5 tablespoons (5 or 6¼T) spinach purée heated with 1 dessertspoon (1T) each, melted butter and cream and a dash of ground nutmeg. While still in the pan, cover half the omelette with spinach, fold over and slide on to a warm plate. Sprinkle with 1 level tablespoon (1¼T) grated Parmesan cheese and serve straight away.

Frittata di patate   Potato omelette

serves 1

Prepare the omelette exactly as described in the recipe for frittata al carciofi.
While still in the pan, cover one half with 4 tablespoons (5T) very creamy mashed potato combined with 1 level dessertspoon (1T) lightly fried onion. Slide out on to a warm plate, sprinkle with 1 level tablespoon (1¼T) grated Parmesan cheese and serve straight away.

Frittata di formaggio   Cheese omelette

serves 1

Prepare the omelette exactly as described in the recipe for frittata al carciofi but add 2 level tablespoons (2½T) grated Parmesan cheese to the beaten eggs.
While still in the pan, sprinkle with a little extra Parmesan cheese. Fold over and slide out on to a warm plate. Serve straight away.

Frittata di cipolla   Onion omelette

serves 1

Fry slowly 1 medium sliced onion in 1 dessertspoon (1T) oil and 1 dessertspoon (1T) melted butter, until soft but not brown.
Prepare an omelette exactly as described in the recipe for frittata al carciofi. While still in the pan, cover one half with the fried onion, fold over and slide out on to a warm plate.
Sprinkle with 1 level tablespoon (1¼T) grated Parmesan cheese and a very light dusting of ground nutmeg. Serve straight away.

Frittata di funghi   Mushroom omelette

serves 1

Prepare the omelette exactly as directed in the previous recipe but first add a good pinch of ground nutmeg to the beaten eggs.
While still in the omelette pan, fill with 2 oz. (⅝ cup) sliced mushrooms, first fried in a little butter. Fold the omelette over, slide on to a warm plate and sprinkle with 1 level tablespoon (1¼T) grated Parmesan cheese. Serve straight away.

Frittatine imbottite   Meat stuffed pancakes

**4 oz. (½ cup) plain
(all-purpose) flour
1 level teaspoon salt
1 egg
1 dessertspoon (1T) olive oil
½ pint (1¼ cups) milk
olive oil
filling as given for cannelloni
(see page 49)
4 level tablespoons (5T) grated
Parmesan cheese
1 oz. (2T) butter
¼ pint (⅝ cup) chicken
or beef stock**

serves 4

Sift the flour and salt into a bowl. Add the unbeaten egg, oil and half
the milk. Beat briskly until smooth and creamy. Stir in the rest of the
milk, then cover the batter and leave to stand for 15 minutes.
Brush a heavy frying pan with oil and heat until hot. Pour in
sufficient batter to cover the base of the pan thinly. Fry until the
underside is golden then turn over and fry the other side. Repeat,
using the rest of the batter (8 pancakes).
Fill the pancakes with the meat mixture, roll up and place in a
well-buttered heatproof dish. Sprinkle with cheese, dot with flakes
of butter then pour the stock into the dish. Cook, uncovered, in the
centre of a moderately hot oven (400°F, Mark 6) for about 15 minutes.
Serve straight away.

Crespolini Spinach and cheese pancakes

4 oz. (½ cup) plain
(all-purpose) flour
1 level teaspoon salt
1 egg
1 dessertspoon (1T) olive oil
½ pint (1¼ cups) milk
olive oil
⅔ teacup (½ cup) thick
spinach purée
⅔ teacup (½ cup) Ricotta cheese
(or cottage cheese)
1 egg
2–3 chicken livers, finely chopped
butter
salt and pepper to taste
nutmeg
1 oz. (2T) butter
2 level tablespoons (2½T) flour
½ pint milk
3–6 level tablespoons (3¾–5T)
grated Parmesan cheese
Mozzarella cheese
butter

serves 4

These are pancakes stuffed handsomely with a combination of cheese, chicken liver and spinach, then coated with sauce. Extremely rich but, at the same time, extremely good.

Cook the pancakes as directed in the previous recipe and stack, one on top of the other, in a tea towel while preparing the filling and sauce.

Combine the purée with the Ricotta cheese (or cottage cheese rubbed through a sieve), egg and butter-fried chicken livers. Season well to taste with salt and pepper and a dash of nutmeg.

Put equal amounts of filling on to each pancake, roll up and cut each into 3 triangles. Arrange in 4 well-buttered individual heatproof dishes.

Make a well-flavoured white sauce with ½ pint (1¼ cups) milk. Add the grated Parmesan cheese and stir until melted.

Pour equal amounts over pancakes in dishes, cover with thin slices of Mozzarella cheese and flakes of butter then re-heat in centre of hot oven (425°F, Mark 7) for 15 to 20 minutes. Serve straight away.

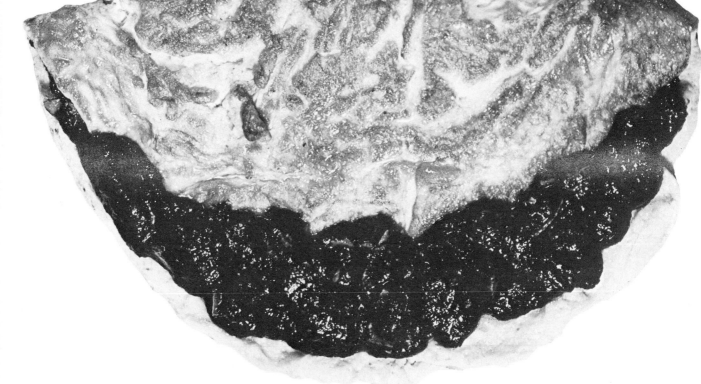

Spinach omelette

Fish

Fish in Italy is treated simply and with respect and is either fried, grilled, poached or stewed. Lemon is well liked as an accompaniment, but involved and creamy sauces—so important to the French—are not, although occasionally fish is served with garlic or tomato sauce or with salsa verda (green sauce) consisting of a basic oil and lemon juice dressing with additions of garlic, anchovies, parsley and capers.

Grilled trout

Fritto misto di mare   Mixed fried fish

¾ lb. white fish (sole, halibut,
turbot or plaice)
¾ lb. shellfish (mussels, prawns,
lobster, pre-cooked ink-fish,
oysters etc.)
1–2 courgettes (zucchine)
4 artichoke hearts, halved
8 mushrooms
4 oz. (½ cup) plain
(all-purpose) flour
1 egg
1 tablespoon (1¼T) olive oil
¼ pint (⅝ cup) milk
salt and pepper to taste
oil
lemon wedges
serves 4

There are many varieties of fritto misto in Italy which consist, in
the main, of small pieces of food dipped in coating batter and then
deep fried in hot oil. Fritto misto mare is basically a fish version.
Again, it is difficult to be strictly authentic with the recipe because
of the unavailability of Mediterranean and Adriatic fish but this
adaptation gives a reasonable result and is worth trying.

Cut the fish into fairly small pieces. Slice the courgettes (zucchini)
and halve the artichoke hearts.
Prepare a fritter batter by beating together until smooth the sifted
flour, 1 egg, olive oil, milk and salt and pepper to taste.
Coat the prepared food with batter then fry in deep hot oil until
crisp and golden. Drain carefully on paper towels then serve hot
with wedges of lemon.

Scampi fritti   Fried scampi

Allow at least 1 lb. scampi or Dublin Bay prawns for 4 people
(shelled weight).
Prepare a batter as directed for fritto misto mare. Coat the prawns
with the batter then fry and serve hot with wedges of lemon.

Scampi fritti e impanati   Egg and crumbed fried scampi

Dust the scampi lightly with well-seasoned flour then coat with
beaten egg and fine breadcrumbs. Fry and serve as above.

Fried scampi

Anguilla alla Fiorentina
Eels Florentine

1½ lb. fresh eel
2 oz. (1 cup) fresh white breadcrumbs
¼ level teaspoon dried sage or double quantity of fresh sage
salt and pepper to taste
6 tablespoons (7½T) olive oil
3 garlic cloves, finely chopped
2 bay leaves
¼ pint (⅝ cup) dry white wine

serves 4

Wash the eels and cut into 2-inch pieces. Dry on paper towels. Combine the breadcrumbs with sage and plenty of freshly ground pepper and salt to taste. Coat the pieces of eel very thoroughly with the crumbs.
Heat the oil in a large frying pan. Add the garlic and bay leaves and cook very gently for 3 minutes. Add the pieces of eel and fry a little more briskly until crisp.
Remove to a heatproof baking dish. Coat with the oil and garlic from the frying pan but discard the bay leaves. Pour the wine into the dish then cook, uncovered, in the centre of a moderate oven (350°F, Mark 4) for 35 to 40 minutes, turning the eels over once. Serve with crusty bread.

Anguilla coi piselli
Braised eel

Prepare exactly as previous recipe but add 6 oz. (1 cup) shelled peas to the pan with the tomato concentrate, water and wine.

Anguilla in umido al vino bianco
Eels in white wine

1½ lb. fresh eels
4 tablespoons (5T) olive oil
1 small onion, finely chopped
1 garlic clove, finely chopped
1 × 2-inch strip of lemon peel
1 level teaspoon chopped fresh sage or ¼ level teaspoon dried sage
1 level tablespoon (1¼T) tomato concentrate
4 tablespoons (5T) warm water
1 wineglass dry white wine
salt and pepper to taste

serves 4

Clean the eels then cut into 2-inch pieces. Dry on paper towels. Heat the oil in a saucepan. Add the onion and garlic and fry very gently until the palest gold. Add the eel and fry until golden all over. Add the lemon peel and sage, then put in the tomato concentrate blended with the water and wine. Season to taste with salt and pepper then simmer gently, uncovered, for approximately 20 minutes or until the fish is tender and most of the liquid has evaporated.

Pesce marinato alla griglia
Marinated grilled fish

4 fish steaks
6 tablespoons (7½T) olive oil
1 finely chopped garlic clove
juice of 1 lemon
2 level teaspoons chopped fresh herbs such as basil, mint, thyme, parsley or sage
salt and pepper to taste

serves 4

Wipe the fish steaks dry with paper towels.
To make the marinade, beat together all the remaining ingredients and put into an enamel or glass dish. Add the fish and turn in the marinade so that both sides are well coated. Cover and leave at room temperature for 1 hour, turning once.
Place fish steaks in an oiled and preheated grill pan and grill for 6 to 8 minutes, brushing frequently with the marinade. Turn over and grill for a further 5 to 6 minutes, brushing with the marinade. Serve hot with wedges of lemon.

Sogliola alla griglia   Grilled sole

Allow 4 whole soles per person and have them skinned on both sides. Place them, 2 at a time, in the preheated grill pan heavily brushed with melted butter. Brush the soles with more butter, sprinkle with salt and pepper and grill for 5 to 6 minutes. Turn over, brush with more butter, and grill for a further 5 to 6 minutes, depending on thickness. Serve straight away with wedges of lemon and savoury butter pats.

Sogliole al marsala   Sole with marsala

8 sole fillets
4 level tablespoons (5T) flour,
well-seasoned with salt
and pepper
2 oz. (¼ cup) butter
1 dessertspoon (1T) olive oil
4 tablespoons (5T) Marsala
4 tablespoons (5T) double
(heavy) cream
1 level tablespoon (1¼T) parsley
serves 4

Dust the sole fillets with the flour. Put the butter into a large frying pan with the oil and heat until both are hot. Add the sole and fry for about 5 to 6 minutes, turning once. Transfer to a warm platter and keep hot.
Add the Marsala, cream and parsley to the pan and shake gently until the sauce is well blended and hot. Pour over the fish and serve straight away.

Filleting fish

Sogliole alla Parmigiana   Sole Parmesan

Prepare 8 fillets of sole as above and fry briskly until golden brown on both sides.
Shake some grated Parmesan cheese over the soles then add 2 tablespoons (2½T) cream and 4 tablespoons (5T) chicken stock (beaten together) to the pan. Cover and simmer for a further 5 minutes. Sprinkle lightly with parsley and serve straight away.

serves 4

Pesce all'agliata   Fish steaks with garlic sauce

1 oz. (½ cup) breadcrumbs
2–3 garlic cloves
1–2 dessertspoons (1–2T) lemon juice
salt and pepper
olive oil
4 fish steaks
flour
serves 4

Put the breadcrumbs into a bowl with the crushed garlic cloves, lemon juice and salt and pepper to taste. Beat with a wooden spoon until smooth, then very gradually beat in olive oil until the sauce is creamy in texture.
Dust the fish steaks with flour and grill or fry until cooked through and golden on both sides. Drain on paper towels and serve straight away with the garlic sauce.

Pesce bollito con salsa verde   Boiled fish with garlic sauce

Because the garlic sauce tends to be rich, we prefer poached fish steaks to fried.
Simply boil, for 15 minutes, 1 whole onion and 1 sliced carrot in a frying pan containing salted water, a few tablespoons dry white wine, a scraping of nutmeg, a short strip of lemon peel and freshly ground pepper. Add the fish then reduce the heat so that water bubbles gently. Cover and simmer for 7 to 10 minutes, depending on the thickness of the fish steaks.
Remove from the pan with a perforated fish slice and serve straight away with the sauce.

serves 4

Tonno alla livornese   Tuna in tomato sauce

Alas, fresh tuna or tunny does not grace our shores and therefore we must settle for the canned variety which—excellent in texture and flavour though it is—doesn't quite match up to the delicacy of freshly caught and freshly cooked tuna. Be that as it may, a couple of cans of middle cut tuna, combined with tomato sauce and served with a dish of buttered pasta is relatively easy to prepare and makes an ample and tasty meal for four, a useful recipe to have up one's sleeve if time is short or if one is suddenly confronted with unexpected guests.
Make up the Neapolitan sauce as given in the recipe for spaghetti neapolitan, page 42.
After it has simmered for the required amount of time, add to it 2 cans of tuna—broken up into largish chunks—and the oil from the cans. Heat through for about 7 to 10 minutes but no longer, or the fish will collapse. Serve over portions of freshly cooked pasta, coated with butter.

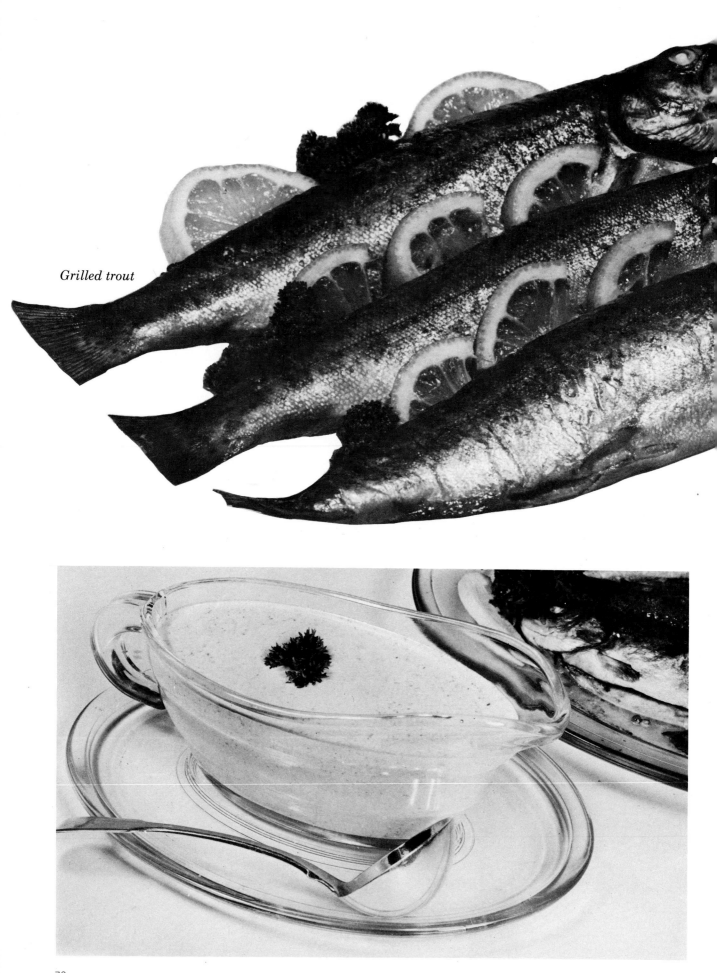

Grilled trout

Trote Trout

One of my happiest moments in Italy was being presented, late one afternoon, with four outsize trout caught by my husband and son on one of their lone pilgrimages to the lakes. The locals advised us to boil them quickly in salted water, smother them with butter and eat them straight away. No more ceremony than that and no other adornments other than some mellow white wine as an accompanying drink. Of course the trout were memorable and how often since have I longed for those same, delicate fish with their unrivalled flavour and soft creamy texture. Poaching is not always the best method of cooking trout and even the Italians tend to grill or fry them if the fish are smaller than average and from yesterday's catch.

Trote alla griglia Grilled trout

Allow 1 trout per person. To grill, have them cleaned but see that the heads are left on.
Wash them thoroughly then dry on paper towels. Place in a well-buttered preheated grill pan and brush with melted butter. Grill for 6 to 8 minutes, depending on thickness. Turn over, brush with more butter and grill for a further 6 to 8 minutes.
Serve straight away and accompany either with extra melted butter or with salsa verde (green sauce) dressing.

Trote fritte Fried trout

Allow 1 trout per person. Prepare as in previous recipe then dust the trouts with well-seasoned flour.
Fry in about 1-inch of melted butter and olive oil mixed, allowing 8 to 10 minutes and turning once. Drain on paper towels and serve with wedges of lemon and salsa verde.

Salsa verde Green garlic sauce

4 tablespoons (5T) olive oil
2 tablespoons (2½T) lemon juice
1 small garlic clove,
finely chopped
3 fillets of anchovy, very
finely chopped
2 level dessertspoons (2T)
capers, drained and chopped
freshly ground pepper to taste

Combine all the ingredients and beat until the dressing thickens slightly and forms an emulsion.

Green garlic sauce

Meat and Poultry

All meat and poultry dishes are noteworthy and while the Italians specialize in, or are most well known for, the way they handle veal, they are just as successful with other meats. Their roast lamb with garlic and rosemary, their Florentine steaks, beef stuffato, chicken cacciatore and duckling elegantly roasted with sage and garlic, are just a few of the specialities which are outstanding and absolutely delicious.

Scaloppine di vitello al Marsala
Veal escalopes with Marsala

1 lb. veal escalopes
flour, well-seasoned with salt
and pepper
3 oz. (⅜ cup) butter
1 dessertspoon (1T) olive oil
1 wineglass Marsala

serves 4

A simple but exceedingly good veal dish.

Cut the veal into very thin slices, then beat each until paper thin.
Coat with flour.
Heat the butter and oil in a large pan and add the slices of veal.
Brown quickly on both sides. Add the Marsala then simmer,
uncovered, for 3 minutes.
Serve immediately and accompany with broccoli and baby potatoes
tossed in butter.

Scaloppine di vitello con sugo di pomodoro
Veal escalopes with tomato sauce

Prepare a tomato sauce as for spaghetti Neapolitan (see page 42).
Fry the veal as directed in the previous recipe but omit the
Marsala. Transfer the veal to 4 individual plates then coat with the
sauce. Serve straight away.

Costelette di vitello alla Milanese
Veal cutlets Milanese

4 best quality veal cutlets
1 egg, beaten
fine white breadcrumbs
4 oz. (½ cup) clarified butter
1 tablespoon (1¼T) olive oil
wedges of lemon for serving

serves 4

These are made from veal cutlets—or veal chops—comprising both
meat and bone. The cutlets should be large, cut fairly thinly and
cooked in clarified butter or olive oil. Although it sounds simple, the
dish can be disastrous if the meat is tough, if coarse crumbs are used
for coating and if anything other than butter and oil is used for
frying. Instructions for clarifying butter are given after the veal
recipe.

Beat the cutlets until as thin as possible. Coat them with the egg then
toss in the crumbs.
Heat the butter and oil in a large frying pan. Add the cutlets, 2 at a
time, and fry briskly on both sides until crisp and golden. Lower the
heat and fry a little more slowly for about 7 minutes or until the
cutlets are cooked through.
Remove from the pan and serve straight away with wedges of lemon.

to clarify butter: melt 4 oz. (½ cup) butter slowly in a saucepan.
Leave to stand for 5 minutes.
Gently pour the butter into a clean bowl, leaving the sediment
behind in the saucepan. Alternatively, strain the butter through
muslin into a clean bowl.

Scaloppe Milanese
Veal escalopes Milanese

Make exactly as directed in the previous recipe but use
4 escalopes of veal instead of cutlets.
Make sure the escalopes are beaten until wafer thin, then snip
round the edge of each with kitchen scissors to prevent them from
curling as they cook.

Scaloppine fredde
Cold veal escalopes

Cook as above, drain thoroughly on paper towels and leave until
cold. Serve with salad.

Costolette bolognese Veal escalopes bolognese

A rich and gratifying combination from Bologna.
Fry the veal escalopes as directed, but for 5 minutes only then
return all four to the pan.
Cover each with a slice of the mildest lean ham available, then
sprinkle with grated Parmesan cheese. Top with flakes of butter,
cover the pan and cook for 3 to 4 minutes or until the cheese melts.
Serve straight away.

Scaloppine di vitello Torinese Veal escalopes Torinese

A variation on the basic veal escalope theme which is said to come
from Turin.
Coat 4 veal escalopes (see veal escalopes Milanese, page 74) with
beaten egg, then toss in a mixture of breadcrumbs and grated
Parmesan cheese.
Fry as directed then top each with anchovy fillets and fresh tomato
slices.

Scaloppine al Marsala con panna Veal with Marsala and cream

1 lb. veal escalopes
flour, well-seasoned with salt
and pepper
3 oz. (⅜ cup) butter
1 tablespoon (1¼T) olive oil
4 oz. (1¼ cups) sliced
mushrooms
1 wine glass Marsala
¼ pint (⅝ cup) double
(heavy) cream
salt and pepper to taste
serves 4

Cut the veal into very thin slices then beat each until paper thin.
Coat with flour.
Heat the butter and oil in a large frying pan. Add the mushrooms
and fry fairly briskly for 2 to 3 minutes. Move to one side of pan.
Add the slices of veal and brown quickly on both sides. Add the
Marsala then simmer, uncovered, for 3 minutes. Transfer to a warm
serving dish and keep hot.
Add the cream to the remaining oil in the pan and heat through
without boiling. Pour on to the veal and serve straight away.

Spezzatino di vitello Veal stew

1–1½ lb. stewing veal
1 oz. (2T) butter
1 tablespoon (1¼T) olive oil
1 garlic clove, finely chopped
1 medium onion, finely chopped
4 tomatoes, skinned and
chopped
¼ pint (⅝ cup) dry white wine
1 level dessertspoon (1T)
tomato concentrate
1 teacup (¾ cup) finely
chopped parsley
1 level teaspoon chopped fresh
basil or half the amount, dried
1 red or green pimento,
de-seeded and chopped
2 medium celery stalks, chopped
salt and pepper to taste
serves 4

Cut the veal into cubes.
Heat the butter and oil in a saucepan. Add the garlic and onion and
fry over a low heat until soft but not brown. Add the veal cubes and
fry a little more briskly until well sealed and brown.
Add the tomatoes, wine, tomato concentrate, parsley, basil, red or
green pimento, celery, and salt and pepper to taste. Bring to the boil,
lower the heat and cover the pan. Simmer for 1½ to 2 hours or until
the veal is very tender.
Serve with noodles tossed in butter and either a salad or green
vegetables.

Braciolette ripiene Anchovy stuffed veal rolls

4 veal escalopes
Mozzarella cheese
4 anchovy fillets
pepper
2 oz. (¼ cup) butter
¼ pint (⅝ cup) dry white wine
2 level tablespoons (2½T) chopped parsley

serves 4

Beat the veal escalopes until very thin. Cover each with thin slices of cheese then place the anchovy fillets on top. Sprinkle with pepper. Roll up (cheese side inside), and hold in place by tying with fine string or thick thread.
Heat the butter in a fairly shallow pan. Add the veal rolls and fry briskly until golden brown all over. Pour the wine into the pan, cover and simmer for 10 minutes.
Transfer the veal rolls to a warm dish and remove the string or thread. Coat with juices from the pan then sprinkle with parsley.

Saltimbocca Ham and veal olives

8 very thin slices of veal, each
6×4-inch
8 very thin slices of ham, each
6×4-inch
8 fresh sage leaves or ½ level
teaspoon dried sage
pepper
2 oz. (¼ cup) butter
1 wineglass dry white wine

serves 4

Another well known veal dish which is said to be of Roman origin.

Cover the slices of veal with ham, then arrange a sage leaf—or sprinkling of dried sage—on each. Sprinkle with pepper. Roll up then hold in place by spearing with cocktail sticks.
Heat the butter in a fairly shallow pan. Add the veal rolls and fry until golden brown.
Pour the wine into the pan. Bring it to the boil then lower the heat. Cover the pan and simmer gently for 10 minutes.
Transfer the veal rolls to a warm dish and remove the cocktail sticks. Coat with the juices from the pan and serve straight away.

L'Osso buco Stewed shin of veal

3–4 lb. shin of veal (veal shank)
flour
6 tablespoons (7½T) olive oil
1 medium onion, thinly sliced
1 medium carrot, grated
1 medium celery stalk, chopped
8 tomatoes, skinned and
chopped
1 level tablespoon (1¼T) tomato
concentrate
¼ pint (⅝ cup) white wine
¼ pint (⅝ cup) chicken or
beef stock
salt and pepper to taste
topping
1 teacup (⅔ cup) finely
chopped parsley
1 garlic clove, chopped
finely grated peel of 1
small lemon

serves 4

A flavourful, colourful veal stew from Milan, always served with risotto Milanese. To be on the safe side, order the cut veal from the butcher in advance, for shin of veal is not always available.

Ask your butcher to saw the veal shin into 3-inch pieces. Coat the pieces in flour.
Heat the oil in a large shallow pan. Add the veal pieces, a few at a time, and fry until well browned. Remove to a plate. Add the onion, carrot and celery to the remaining oil in the pan and fry slowly until soft but not brown.
Stir in the tomatoes, tomato concentrate, wine, stock and salt and pepper to taste. Bring to the boil. Replace the veal, lower the heat and cover the pan. Simmer very gently until tender, allowing 1½ to 2 hours.
Turn out on to a warm dish then sprinkle with topping ingredients mixed well together.

Vitello tonnato Veal with tuna sauce

1½ lb. cold roast veal,
preferably boneless
½ pint (1¼ cups) thick home-
made mayonnaise
1 can (7 oz.) middle cut tuna,
finely mashed with its oil
juice of ½ a lemon
8 anchovy fillets, finely chopped
veal or chicken stock
pepper to taste
1 level tablespoon (1¼T) finely
chopped capers (optional)
wedges of lemon for garnishing

serves 6–8

A blissful dish for hot summer days. It may be made in advance and refrigerated overnight.

Slice the cold veal fairly thinly and arrange on a large serving dish. Combine the mayonnaise with the tuna, lemon juice and anchovies, then thin down to the consistency of cream with the cold stock.
Season to taste with pepper and stir in the capers.
Spoon the sauce over the veal, making sure the meat is completely covered. Chill for up to 12 hours. Before serving, garnish with wedges of lemon.

Anchovy stuffed veal rolls

Arrosto di agnello — Roast lamb

1 medium sized leg of lamb (about 4 lb.)
2 medium garlic cloves, peeled and cut into slivers
1 level teaspoon dried rosemary or 1 dessertspoon (1T) fresh
3 oz. (⅜ cup) melted butter
pepper and salt
¼ pint (⅝ cup) dry red wine
serves 6–8

Wash the lamb and pat dry with paper towels.

Make incisions in the lamb flesh and insert slivers of garlic and rosemary.

Place in a roasting tin. Coat with the melted butter and any left-over rosemary. Put into a preheated oven (425°F, Mark 7) and roast for 15 minutes. Sprinkle with salt and pepper.

Reduce the temperature to moderate (350°F, Mark 4) and continue to roast for a further 1½ hours.

Pour the wine over the meat and roast for a further 15 minutes, basting frequently. Remove the lamb to a carving board.

Skim off the fat from the pan juices then heat the juices until thick and syrupy.

To serve the lamb, cut it into thick slices and accompany with the juices.

Arrosto al Marsala — Roast lamb with Marsala

Prepare exactly as above, using Marsala instead of red wine.

Maiale alla Napoletana   Pork Neapolitan

Neapolitan sauce, (see
spaghetti Neapolitan, page 42)
4 pork chops
1 cut clove garlic
flour
2 tablespoons (2½T) olive oil
½ level teaspoon dried sage or
1 level teaspoon fresh
chopped sage
salt and pepper to taste

Arrange the sauce over the base of a heatproof dish.
Rub the chops with the cut clove of garlic, then coat with flour. Fry briskly in the hot olive oil until crisp and golden on both sides.
Place in the dish on top of the sauce, then sprinkle with sage and salt and pepper to taste. Cover and cook in the centre of a preheated moderate oven (350°F, Mark 4) for 30 minutes.

Fritto misto Milanese   Mixed fried meat Milanese

Make as fritto misto mare (page 66) but instead of fish, use 1 lb. escalopes of veal and ½ lb. (1 cup) chicken livers, both cut into fairly small pieces. Also include florets of cooked cauliflower.

Mixed fried meat milanese

Roast lamb

Roast pork Florentine style

Arrosto di maiale alla Fiorentina

Roast pork Florentine style

3 to 4 lb. loin of pork
2 garlic cloves, cut into slivers
1 level teaspoon fresh or ½ level teaspoon dried rosemary
4 cloves
5 tablespoons (6¼T) water
5 tablespoons (6¼T) red wine
salt and pepper

serves 4–6

Usually roasted in a tin containing water, the flavour of the pork is greatly improved if a little red wine is used in addition.

Ask your butcher to score the skin by cutting into lines about ⅛-inch apart.
Make incisions in the flesh of the joint, then insert slivers of garlic and rosemary into each. Press the cloves into the meat then place the joint in a roasting tin containing the water and wine.
Sprinkle heavily with salt and lightly with pepper. Roast in a moderate oven (350°F, Mark 4) for 2 to 2½ hours or until the meat is very tender but still moist. Baste occasionally.

Bistecca alla Fiorentina
Steak Florentine

I remember buying my first Florentine steaks in a supermarket in Viareggio and being staggered by their immense size—and price! They were mammoth affairs—closely resembling the American T-bone rib steaks—moist, tender and succulent and perhaps the finest tasting beef I have ever eaten. Being a speciality from Tuscany, the cut is obviously hard to find elsewhere but T-bone steaks, rubbed with a cut clove of garlic, brushed with oil and grilled, make an admirable substitute.

Bistecca alla pizzaiola
Beefsteak Neapolitan

Prepare pizzaiola sauce (see macaroni alla pizzaiola, page 43).
Grill 4 rump steaks according to taste (rare, medium or well cooked). Arrange on warm plates then top with the sauce. Serve straight away.

Stufato di manzo
Beef stew

2½ to 3 lb. lean stewing beef
1 level teaspoon salt
good shake pepper
1 small bay leaf, crushed
½ level teaspoon dried thyme
2 medium onions
2 garlic cloves, chopped
1 medium celery stalk, chopped
½ pint (1¼ cups) dry red wine
1 tablespoon (1¼T) olive oil
4 bacon rashers (bacon strips), chopped
½ pint (1¼ cups) beef stock

serves 4

A superior beef stew from the extreme north east, slightly resembling the French Boeuf Bourguigonne.

Cut the beef into 1-inch cubes.
To make a marinade, put the salt, pepper, bay leaf, thyme, 1 sliced onion, garlic, celery and wine into a bowl. Add the cubes of beef, cover the dish and leave to stand in a cold place for 5 to 6 hours. Turn the meat about three times. Before cooking, lift the meat out of the marinade and drain each cube carefully.
Heat the oil in a pan, then add the second onion, finely chopped, and the bacon. Fry gently until soft and pale gold. Add the beef cubes and fry a little more briskly until well sealed and brown.
Strain the marinade into the pan, then add the stock. Slowly bring to the boil. Cover the pan and lower the heat. Simmer gently for 2 to 2½ hours or until the meat is tender and the liquid fairly condensed. Stir occasionally.

Stufatino di manzo alla Romana
Beef stew Roman style

Make exactly as given in the previous recipe but use marjoram instead of thyme and add 2 level dessertspoons (2T) tomato concentrate with the stock.

Mixed fried fish (above)
Grilled trout (below)
Grilled sole (right)
Beef stew (far right)

Braccioli Stuffed meat rolls

6 thin steaks
6 bacon rashers (strips)
2 large onions, finely chopped
2 oz. (¼ cup) butter
2 tablespoons (2½T) oil
6 oz. (3 cups) fresh white breadcrumbs
2 oz. (½ cup) grated Parmesan cheese
1 level teaspoon marjoram
1 oz. (⅛ cup) sultanas
1 oz. (⅛ cup) blanched almonds chopped
1 level teaspoon salt
pepper
3 level tablespoons (3¾T) tomato concentrate
½ pint (1¼ cups) beef stock
seasoning to taste
serves 4

Braccioli are tasty meat rolls filled with an unusual stuffing and then oven-braised in tomato sauce.

Remove excess fat from the meat, then stand the meat on a board and roll with the rolling pin until very thin. Fry the bacon gently for 1 minute on each side then place a rasher on each slice of meat. To make the stuffing, fry the onions gently in butter and 1 tablespoon (1¼T) oil for 3 to 4 minutes. Remove half the onions and keep on one side. Add the crumbs, cheese, marjoram, sultanas, almonds, salt and pepper to the remaining onions and mix well. Divide equally between the meat slices and press down. Roll up tightly and secure the ends with cocktail sticks (picks). To braise, heat the rest of the oil in a large flame-proof casserole and brown the meat rolls evenly on all sides. Add the remaining onion, and tomato concentrate mixed with stock. Season to taste with salt and pepper and bring to the boil. Cover the dish with a lid, then cook in the centre of a cool oven (325°F, Mark 3), for about 1 hour or until the meat is tender.
Serve with freshly cooked pasta, tossed in butter.

Fegato di vitello alla Milanese Liver Milanese

serves 4

Make exactly as veal escalopes Milanese, using 4 large slices of the very best liver (calf's for preference). Cut to about ¼-inch in thickness. Fry for about 5 to 6 minutes, turning once.

Fegato di vitello al Marsala Liver with Marsala and sage

serves 4

Make exactly as veal scallopine with Marsala, but use 4 slices of calf's liver (¼-inch thick) instead of veal. Add 4 chopped sage leaves or ¼ level teaspoon dried sage at the same time as the Marsala.

Trippa alla Fiorentina Tripe Florentine

Tripe is a great favourite with Italians and it is, without doubt, a dish worth sampling when cooked in the Florentine style.

Prepare a Neapolitan sauce, as given in the recipe for spaghetti Neapolitan (page 42), but add 1 to 2 level teaspoons dried rosemary instead of the basil.
Boil 2 lb. dressed tripe in salted water for 10 minutes. Drain and cut into squares. Add to the tomato sauce and simmer for approximately 45 minutes to 1 hour or until the tripe is tender but still fairly firm—rather like pasta. Coat each serving liberally with grated Parmesan cheese and serve straight away.

Trippa alla Parmigiana Buttered tripe with Parmesan cheese

2 lb. dressed tripe
½ pint (1¼ cups) milk
½ pint (1¼ cups) water
1 to 2 level teaspoons salt
3 oz. (⅜ cup) butter
2 oz. (½ cup) grated Parmesan cheese
serves 4

Cut the tripe into strips. Put them into a saucepan with the milk, water and salt. Simmer for about 45 minutes or until the tripe is tender but still firm. Drain.
Melt the butter in a clean saucepan. Add the tripe and fry gently for about 5 minutes. Add the cheese and leave over a low heat until it just begins to melt. Serve straight away.

Veal with tuna sauce (left)

Stuffed aubergines (above)

Veal escalopes torinese (top)

Polpette con sugo di pomodoro
Meat balls with tomato sauce

1 lb. raw minced (ground) beef
2 slices white bread
warm water
2 garlic cloves, chopped
3 level tablespoons (3¾T) finely
chopped parsley
large pinch of nutmeg
salt and pepper to taste
2 eggs, beaten
any of the tomato sauces given
in the pasta section
serves 4

Put the beef into a bowl. Cover the bread with warm water and leave 2 or 3 minutes. Squeeze dry then add the beef with the garlic, parsley, nutmeg, salt and pepper to taste and the beaten eggs. Mix very thoroughly by kneading with the hand. Shape into small balls and drop gently into a pan of hot tomato sauce. Cover and simmer gently for 15 to 20 minutes or until cooked through. Serve with freshly cooked noodles.

Petti di pollo alla Bolognese
Chicken breasts Bolognese

serves 2

Make exactly as veal escalopes Bolognese (page 75) using the raw breast from 1 medium sized roasting (broiling) chicken. To remove the breast, lift away the skin from each side of the breast bone then, using a sharp knife, cut away the flesh completely. Flatten by beating with a rolling pin.

Chicken cacciatora

Pollo alla cacciatora   Chicken cacciatora

1 medium sized roasting (broiling) chicken, jointed
flour
2 oz. (¼ cup) butter
1 tablespoon (1¼T) olive oil
1 large onion, chopped
2 garlic cloves, chopped
8 medium tomatoes, skinned and chopped
3 tablespoons (3¾T) tomato concentrate
1 level teaspoon sugar
¼ pint (⅝ cup) chicken stock
salt and pepper to taste
8 oz. (2½ cups) sliced mushrooms
4 tablespoons (5T) Marsala
serves 4

Coat the chicken joints with flour. Heat the butter and oil in a large pan. Add the chicken joints and fry until crisp and golden. Remove to a plate.

Add the onion and garlic to the pan and fry gently until pale gold. Stir in the tomatoes, tomato concentrate, sugar and stock then season well to taste with salt and pepper. Bring to the boil.

Replace the chicken, cover the pan and simmer slowly for 30 to 45 minutes. Add the mushrooms and Marsala and continue to cook for a further 10 to 15 minutes.

Serve with freshly cooked pasta.

Pollo Marengo   Chicken Marengo

Make as chicken cacciatora in previous recipe but use dry white wine instead of the Marsala. Add 1 level tablespoon (1¼T) tomato concentrate, 4 heaped tablespoons (5½T) parsley and 12 stoned black olives with salt and pepper to taste. Use only half the quantity of mushrooms.

Meat balls with tomato sauce

89

Fried chicken (right)

Stewed shin of veal (below)

Meat balls with tomato sauce
served with tagliatelle (far right)

Veal escalope Bolognese (far right
below)

Pollo fritto Fried chicken

A good way of cooking baby spring chickens which might otherwise
be tasteless.

Cut each chicken into halves or quarters, depending on the size.
If liked, rub the pieces with a cut clove of garlic. Sprinkle with
lemon juice then dust lightly with well-seasoned flour.
Cover a large frying pan with ½-inch of melted butter and olive oil.
Heat until hot then add the pieces of chicken, skin side up. Fry until
golden, turn over and cover the pan. Continue to fry, turning twice,
for a further 20 to 30 minutes or until the chicken is tender.
Remove from the pan, drain on paper towels then serve straight
away with wedges of lemon.

Pollo al vino bianco Chicken in white wine

**1 roasting (broiling) chicken,
weighing about 4 lb.
flour, well-seasoned with salt
and pepper
2 oz. (¼ cup) butter
2 tablespoons (2½T) olive oil
1 medium onion, finely grated
1 garlic clove, finely chopped
2 medium carrots, grated
2 medium celery stalks,
finely chopped
1 slice lean ham, chopped
½ a small lemon
8 oz. (2½ cups) sliced mushrooms
½ pint (1¼ cups) dry white wine
¼ pint (⅝ cup) chicken stock
salt and pepper to taste
½ level teaspoon dried rosemary
or double the amount of fresh**
serves 4

Divide the chicken into joints and dust well with seasoned flour.
Heat the butter and oil in a large pan. Add the chicken joints and fry
until brown and crisp all over. Remove to a plate.
Add the onion, garlic, carrots, celery, and ham and fry over a low
heat until soft but not brown. Add the lemon, mushrooms, wine,
stock, salt and pepper to taste and the rosemary. Bring to the boil
and lower heat.
Replace the chicken, lower the heat and cover the pan. Simmer very
gently for 45 minutes or until the chicken is tender.

Chicken in wine

Coniglio al vino bianco

Rabbit in white wine

serves 4

Cook exactly as directed in previous recipe, using a young jointed rabbit instead of the chicken.

Petti di pollo al Marsala

Fried chicken Marsala

4 breast joints of roasting (broiling) chicken
3 oz. (⅜ cup) butter
1 dessertspoon (1T) olive oil
4 tablespoons (5T) chicken stock
salt and pepper to taste
4 tablespoons (5T) Marsala

serves 4

Wash and dry the joints thoroughly. Heat the butter and oil in a large frying pan. Add the joints, skin side up, and fry until crisp. Turn over and fry the other side until golden and crisp.
Pour the stock into the pan and then sprinkle the joints with salt and pepper. Cover and cook gently for 30 minutes or until the chicken is tender.
Pour the Marsala into the pan. Uncover and continue to simmer until most of the pan juices have evaporated. Serve straight away.

Pollo in padella

Fried chicken with tomatoes and pimentos

Cook the chicken as above.
After 10 minutes, add 4 skinned and chopped tomatoes, 1 de-seeded and coarsely chopped red or green pimento and ½ level teaspoon dried rosemary.
Cover the pan and continue cooking until the chicken is tender.

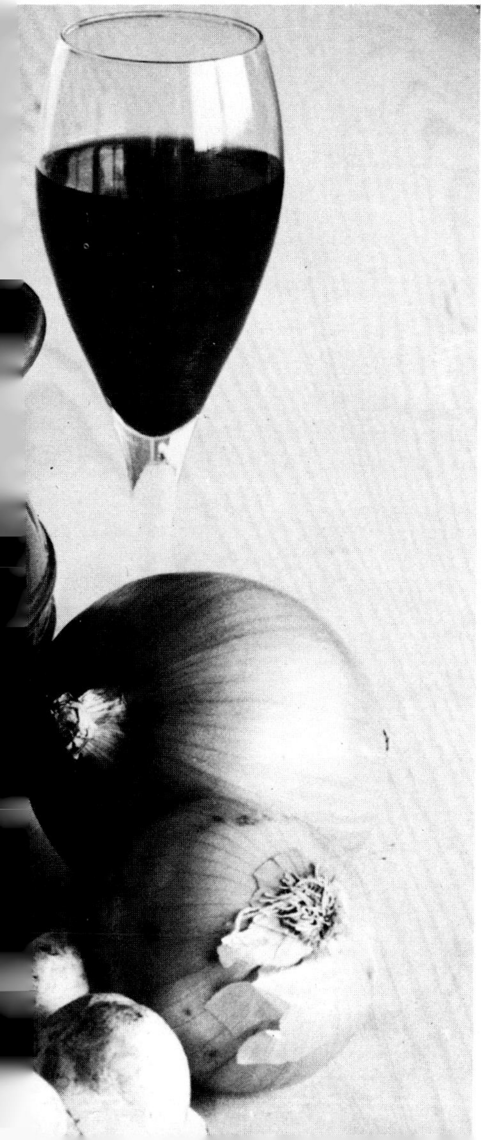

Chicken in wine (above)
Chicken cacciatora (right)
Roast duck (above right)

Pollo al barolo Chicken in wine

1 roasting (broiling) chicken,
weighing about 4 lb.
flour, well-seasoned with salt
and pepper
2 oz. ($\frac{1}{4}$ cup) butter
4 tablespoons (5T) olive oil
1 medium onion, chopped
2 medium carrots, thinly sliced
2 medium celery stalks, chopped
chicken liver, chopped
$\frac{1}{4}$ pint ($\frac{5}{8}$ cup) chicken stock
$\frac{1}{4}$ pint ($\frac{5}{8}$ cup) dry red wine
1 level teaspoon dried basil
4 oz. (1$\frac{1}{4}$ cups) sliced mushrooms
salt and pepper to taste
2 level tablespoons (2$\frac{1}{2}$T) finely
chopped parsley
3 tablespoons (3$\frac{3}{4}$T) Marsala
serves 4

Slightly reminiscent of the French Coq au Vin, this Italian dish is
deliciously flavoured and ideal for dinner parties. It teams well with
pasta or buttered baby potatoes and a fresh green salad.

Divide the chicken into joints and dust each all over with seasoned
flour. Heat the butter and olive oil in a large saucepan. Add the
chicken and brown all over. Remove to a plate.
Add the vegetables and liver to the remaining butter and oil in the
pan then fry slowly until pale gold. Add the stock, wine and basil then
replace the chicken. Cover and cook gently for 30 minutes.
Add all the remaining ingredients then continue to simmer until the
chicken is tender.

Arrosto di anitra Roast duck

1 duckling, about 4 lb. oven-
ready weight
2 fresh sage leaves or $\frac{1}{4}$ level
teaspoon dried sage
1 garlic clove, halved
salt and pepper to taste
5 (6$\frac{1}{4}$T) tablespoons Marsala
serves 4

Wash and wipe the duckling inside and outside with paper towels,
then put the sage and garlic into the body cavity. Place on a grid
resting in a large roasting pan.
Prick the skin all over with a fork, then sprinkle with salt and
pepper. Pour the Marsala into the pan. Roast in the centre of a
moderately hot oven (375°F, Mark 5) for 1$\frac{1}{2}$ hours, basting at least
twice.

95

Vegetables
and Salads

Fresh vegetables are much appreciated by the Italians and they go to some considerable trouble to make them appetizing and flavoursome. Aubergines (eggplants) and courgettes (zucchini) are frequently coated with flour and lightly fried; peas are braised with onions and ham; potatoes are fried with rosemary; mushrooms are stuffed or made into fritters; pimentos are stewed with tomatoes and onions; and very ordinary cabbage, braised with tomatoes, bacon and vinegar, is transformed beyond all recognition.

Italian salads, sometimes served as an hors d'oeuvre and sometimes as an accompaniment to a main course, are always simple, crisp, super-fresh, flavoured with garlic and lightly dressed with oil and vinegar or lemon juice. Of course one finds, all over the country, the green or mixed salad gaily festooned with strips of red and yellow pimento, tomatoes, onion rings and frequently olives. But there are also intriguing combinations of, for example, cucumber with fennel; lightly cooked cauliflower with anchovies, capers and olives; raw mushrooms with seafood. Clever and artistic touches demonstrate imaginative flair and masterly strokes of originality. An approach, in fact, which is very typically Italian.

Melanzane al forno — Baked aubergines (eggplants)

2 medium sized
aubergines (eggplants)
2 garlic cloves, chopped
4 tablespoons (5T) olive oil
½ level teaspoon dried basil or
double that amount of fresh
chopped basil
1 level tablespoon (1¼T)
tomato concentrate
salt and pepper to taste

serves 4

Wash and dry the aubergines (eggplants) and cut in half lengthwise. Score the flesh into a criss cross pattern with a sharp knife.
Beat all the remaining ingredients well together and spread on to the aubergines (eggplants). Transfer to a baking tray and bake in the centre of a moderate oven (350°F, Mark 4) for about 45 minutes or until tender.

Melanzane fritte — Fried aubergines (eggplants)

2 aubergines (eggplants)
salt
flour, seasoned with pepper
deep oil for frying

serves 4

Wash and dry the aubergines (eggplants), then cut into ¼-inch thick slices. Stand on a rack, sprinkle heavily with salt and leave until the water has drained out. (Important to do this otherwise they may become very watery.) Wash and dry very thoroughly then toss in flour well seasoned with pepper.
Heat the oil until a cube of bread dropped into it turns golden in 1 minute and floats to the top. Add the aubergine (eggplant) slices and fry until golden brown. Remove from the pan, drain on soft paper towels and serve straight away.

note: if liked, fried aubergines (eggplants) may be sprinkled with grated Parmesan cheese.

Zucchine fritte — Fried courgettes (zucchini)

serves 4

Prepare exactly as the aubergines (eggplants) in the previous recipe, using 8 medium courgettes (zucchini). Do not peel the courgettes (zucchini) and cut into ¼-inch thick slices before salting.

Sedano al gratin — Celery with cheese sauce

1 large head of celery
1 oz. (2T) butter
2 level tablespoons (2½T) flour
¼ pint (⅝ cup) celery water
¼ pint (⅝ cup) milk
2 oz. (½ cup) grated
Parmesan cheese
salt and pepper to taste
a little extra butter for the top

serves 4

Wash the celery thoroughly and cut into 1-inch lengths. Cook in boiling, salted water until tender but still crisp. Drain, reserving ¼ pint (⅝ cup) water and keep the celery hot.
Melt the butter in a saucepan. Add the flour and cook for 2 minutes without browning. Gradually blend in the celery water and milk. Cook, stirring, until the sauce comes to the boil and thickens, then simmer for 2 minutes. Add half the cheese, then season to taste with salt and pepper.
Put the celery into a buttered heatproof dish then coat with the sauce. Sprinkle the rest of the cheese over the top, then dot with flakes of butter. Brown under a hot grill and serve straight away.

Pisellini dolci al prosciutto — Braised peas

1 oz. (2T) butter
1 medium onion, finely chopped
4 level tablespoons (5T) finely
chopped ham
2 lb. fresh peas
4 tablespoons (5T) water
salt and pepper to taste

serves 4

A Roman dish, delicious made with early summer peas which are delicate and sweet.

Heat the butter in a pan. Add the onion and fry gently, without browning, until soft. Add the ham, peas and water with salt and pepper to taste. Cover tightly and cook slowly for 15 minutes. Uncover and continue to simmer for a further 15 minutes or until most of the liquid has evaporated. Serve straight away.

Crocchette di patate   Potato croquettes

**4 large potatoes
1 oz. (2T) butter
1 oz. (¼ cup) grated
Parmesan cheese
2 egg yolks
large pinch of nutmeg
salt and pepper to taste
2 egg whites
lightly toasted breadcrumbs
deep oil for frying**

serves 4

Peel and wash the potatoes. Cut into quarters and cook in boiling, salted water until soft. Drain, stand the pan of potatoes over the lowest possible heat and mash finely.

Add the butter, cheese, egg yolks, nutmeg and salt and pepper to taste. When the mixture is cool enough to handle, form into croquettes or cork shapes. Coat with lightly beaten egg white and crumbs.

Heat the oil until a cube of bread, dropped into it, turns golden in 1 minute and floats to the top. Add the croquettes and fry until golden. Remove from the pan, drain on soft kitchen paper and serve straight away.

Patate fritte
Fried potatoes with rosemary

2 oz. ($\frac{1}{4}$ cup) butter
2 tablespoons (2$\frac{1}{2}$T) olive oil
4 medium cooked
potatoes, sliced
1 level teaspoon dried rosemary
serves 4

Heat the butter and oil in a frying pan. Add the potato slices then sprinkle with rosemary.
Fry over a medium heat until golden, turning frequently until all the potato slices are evenly browned. Serve straight away.

Fagiolini al burro
Butter fried beans

1 lb. (5 cups) sliced green
(snap) beans
1 oz. (2T) butter
1 tablespoon (1$\frac{1}{4}$T) olive oil
1 garlic clove, finely chopped
salt and pepper to taste
serves 4

Cook the beans in boiling, salted water until just tender. Meanwhile, slowly heat the butter, oil and garlic in a frying pan.
Drain the beans very thoroughly. Add to the pan of butter mixture and heat through for about 5 minutes, turning frequently. Serve straight away.

Fagiolini al pomodoro
Green beans in tomato sauce

Cook the same quantity of green (snap) beans as in the previous recipe, then combine with any of the tomato sauces given in the pasta section.

Cavolo stufato
Braised cabbage

4 oz. (1 cup) bacon,
(coarsely chopped
1 small onion, chopped
1 medium white
cabbage, shredded
4 tomatoes, skinned and chopped
$\frac{1}{4}$ pint ($\frac{5}{8}$ cup) water
salt and pepper to taste
1 tablespoon (1$\frac{1}{4}$T) wine vinegar
serves 4

In a large saucepan, fry the bacon slowly in its own fat until soft. Add the onion and continue to fry for a further 5 minutes or until soft but not brown.
Add all the remaining ingredients and boil for 5 minutes. Lower the heat, stir well to mix, then cover the pan. Simmer gently for 20 minutes, stirring frequently. Serve straight away.

Crema di spinaci
Creamed spinach

1 pint (2$\frac{1}{2}$ cups) spinach purée
5 tablespoons (6$\frac{1}{4}$T) double
(heavy) cream
pinch of ground nutmeg
salt and pepper to taste
serves 4

Put all the ingredients into a saucepan. Heat slowly, stirring frequently until most of the liquid has evaporated. Serve straight away.

Funghi in umido all'aglio
Braised mushrooms with garlic

4 tablespoons (5T) olive oil
2 garlic cloves, finely chopped
1 lb. (5 cups) sliced mushrooms
$\frac{1}{2}$ teaspoon chopped fresh mint
or double the amount of basil
salt and freshly milled pepper
to taste
serves 4

Heat the oil in a large pan, then add the garlic. Fry gently for 5 minutes.
Add all the remaining ingredients, cover the pan and simmer for 15 to 20 minutes.

A selection of vegetables

Peperonata   Peppers, Italian style

6 medium red pimentos
2 large onions
1 garlic clove
12 medium red tomatoes, skinned
5 tablespoons (6¼T) olive oil
salt to taste

A famous stew of pimentos, tomatoes, onions and garlic which is a bit like the Mediterranean ratatouille in character, but less demanding of assorted vegetables and easier to make. It is one of those concoctions which improves on keeping and reheating and therefore it makes sense to double or even treble the quantities given below.

De-seed the pimentos and cut into strips. Slice the onions thinly. Chop the garlic and tomatoes.
Heat the oil in a large pan. Add the pimentos, onions and garlic. Fry gently for 15 minutes. Add the tomatoes and salt to taste. Cover and simmer for 30 minutes.

serves 4—6

Fritelle di funghi   Mushroom fritters

serves 4

Make a fritter batter as for fritto misto mare (page 68). Coat about 12 oz. (3¾ cups) sliced or whole mushrooms in batter and fry in deep hot oil until crisp and golden. Remove from the pan, drain on soft paper towels and sprinkle with salt and pepper. If liked, the fried mushrooms may also be sprinkled with grated Parmesan cheese.

Mushroom fritters (above left)   *Stuffed mushrooms (above right)*

Funghi ripieni   Stuffed mushrooms

16 large mushrooms
4 level tablespoons (5T) soft
white breadcrumbs
1 medium onion, grated
1 small garlic clove, chopped
1 level tablespoon (1¼T) finely
chopped parsley
3 anchovy fillets, finely chopped
4 tablespoons (5T) olive oil
beaten egg
freshly ground pepper

serves 4

A speciality from the Piedmont region.

Remove the mushroom stalks and chop finely. Place the mushrooms on a lightly buttered baking tray.

Put the chopped stalks into a bowl and add the breadcrumbs, onion, garlic, parsley, anchovies and 1 tablespoon (1¼T) olive oil. Bind with a little beaten egg, then season to taste with pepper.

Pile equal amounts on to the mushrooms, then spoon the remaining oil over each. Cover with foil and cook in the centre of a moderate oven (350°F, Mark 4) for 30 minutes.

note: aubergines (eggplants) can be stuffed in the same way, with the stuffing varied.

Asparagi alla Parmigiana
Asparagus with butter and Parmesan cheese

serves 4

Wash and scrape about 2 lb. of asparagus then cut off the tough part of the stalks. Tie in bundles and cook in boiling (unsalted) water for about 15 to 20 minutes or until tender.
Drain and arrange on a warm plate. Sprinkle with grated Parmesan cheese, then coat heavily with melted butter. Serve straight away.

Insalata verde
Lettuce salad

1 cut clove garlic
1 large lettuce
4 tablespoons (5T) olive oil
1 tablespoon (1¼T) lemon juice
1 tablespoon (1¼T) wine vinegar
salt and pepper to taste
serves 4

Rub the salad bowl with the cut clove of garlic. Wash the lettuce and shake the leaves dry. Tear into bite-size pieces and put into the salad bowl.
Sprinkle the lettuce with all the remaining ingredients. Toss thoroughly but gently and serve straight away.

Insalata di cavalfiore
Cauliflower salad

1 medium cauliflower
8 anchovy fillets, finely chopped
18 ripe black olives, stoned and halved
1 small onion, grated
1 level tablespoon (1¼T) capers
6 tablespoons (7½T) olive oil
2 tablespoons (2½T) lemon juice
1 tablespoon (1¼T) wine vinegar
freshly milled pepper to taste
serves 4–6

Break the cauliflower into florets and cook in boiling, salted water for 5 minutes. Drain and transfer to a bowl. Cool to lukewarm, then refrigerate for at least 1 hour.
Put all the remaining ingredients into a bowl. Add the chilled cauliflower and toss thoroughly. Chill for a further 30 minutes before serving.

Insalata di finocchi e cetrioli
Fennel and cucumber salad

1 clove garlic
1 medium cucumber
1 bulb of fennel
4 tablespoons (5T) olive oil
2 tablespoons (2½T) lemon juice
salt and freshly milled pepper to taste
serves 4–6

Rub the cut clove of garlic round the inside of a salad bowl. Peel the cucumber and slice thinly. Wash and dry the fennel and grate coarsely. Put both into the salad bowl.
Beat the remaining ingredients well together and add to the salad. Toss thoroughly and serve straight away.

Insalata mista   Mixed salad

1 garlic clove
1 medium cucumber
4 medium tomatoes, skinned
1 medium carrot
1 medium onion
1 head of chicory
4 tablespoons (5T) thick mayonnaise
2 tablespoons (2½T) olive oil
1 tablespoon (1¼T) lemon juice
1 tablespoon (1¼T) wine vinegar
serves 4

Rub the salad bowl with the cut clove of garlic.
Peel and slice the cucumber. Cut the tomatoes into wedges. Dice the carrot. Grate the onion coarsely. Discard the outer leaves of the chicory, then gently pull off the remaining leaves. Put all the prepared vegetables into the salad bowl.
Beat the remaining ingredients well together. Pour over the salad and toss thoroughly.

Tomato salad

Insalata di pomodori   Tomato salad

8 large tomatoes, skinned
olive oil
salt and pepper to taste
2 heaped tablespoons (2¾T)
finely chopped fresh basil or
½ level teaspoon dried
1 small onion, finely grated
serves 4

Slice the tomatoes and arrange in a single layer on a large flat platter. Sprinkle with all the remaining ingredients and serve straight away.

Salad ingredients (previous page)

Seafood salad with mushrooms

Insalata di fagiolini   Green bean salad

1 garlic clove
1 lb. (2½ cups) sliced green
(snap) beans, cooked
3 tablespoons (3¾T) olive oil
2 tablespoons (2½T) lemon juice
salt and pepper to taste
serves 4

Rub the inside of a salad bowl with the cut clove of garlic.
Add the beans, oil and lemon juice. Sprinkle to taste with salt and pepper, toss thoroughly and serve straight away.

Insalata di funghi e frutti di mare   Seafood salad with mushrooms

1 garlic clove
8 oz. (2½ cups) sliced mushrooms
8 oz. (2 cups) chopped scampi
or lobster
4 tablespoons (5T) olive oil
2 tablespoons (2½T) lemon juice
salt and pepper
2 level tablespoons (2½T) finely
chopped parsley
serves 4

Rub the salad bowl with the cut clove of garlic.
Put all the remaining ingredients into the bowl and toss lightly together. Serve straight away.

Desserts

The Italian has, by nature, a sweet tooth and loves his rich, liqueur-laden, outsize wedge of cake accompanied by a miniature cup of heavy, black coffee. Or his giant portion of ice cream. Or his almond macaroons (an Italian invention), assorted biscuits and sweet pastries. But not after a meal. Indeed, the dessert course in the average Italian home consists of little more than fresh fruit or a piece of cheese, and the pie and pudding as we know it has never been appreciated by the Italians. For family festivities and special occasions, a cake will be bought from the local cake shop and served with Marsala or a liqueur at the end of a meal or Mama will make zabaglione, trifle, fresh fruit salad, water ice or a confection of puréed chestnuts with rum, vanilla, cream and chocolate. But this remains an occasional happening and, for the most part, the Italian is happy enough to enjoy his sweetmeats in any one of the restaurants or coffee bars to be found in every nook and cranny of the country.

Italian trifle

Zuppa inglese Italian trifle

8 large macaroons
8 tablespoons (10T) Marsala
1 level teaspoon finely grated
orange peel
¾ pint (2 cups) milk
4 eggs, beaten
3 level tablespoons (3¾T)
vanilla sugar
¾ pint (2 cups) double
(heavy) cream
3 tablespoons (3¾T) milk
2 level tablespoons (2½T) blanched
and chopped pistachio
nuts or flaked and
toasted almonds
serves 6–8

An exceedingly sumptuous and rich trifle-de-luxe.

Break up the macaroons and put into a serving bowl. Moisten with the Marsala, then sprinkle with orange peel.
Bring the milk just up to the boil then pour, with the eggs and sugar, into a basin standing on a saucepan of gently simmering water. Cook, stirring frequently, until the custard thickens sufficiently to coat the back of a spoon, but on no account allow the custard to boil or it will curdle. Pour into a clean bowl (to prevent further cooking), leave the custard until cold, then pour into the dish over the macaroons.
Beat the cream and milk together until softly stiff, then pile over the custard. Scatter the nuts on top and serve straight away.

Zabaglione (left)

Zabaglione

Zabaglione   Zabaglione

6 egg yolks
4 level tablespoons (5T)
castor sugar
1 large wine glass Marsala

Put the egg yolks and sugar into a basin standing over a saucepan of very gently boiling water. Whisk until thick and white.
Still whisking, add the Marsala gradually. Continue whisking until the zabaglione thickens and becomes light and foamy.
Pour into glasses and serve straight away.

serves 4

note: do not allow zabaglione to boil or it will curdle.

Pesche ripiene in vino bianco   Stuffed peaches in wine

4 large Italian peaches
1½ oz. (¾ cup) crushed
macaroon crumbs
1 oz. (½ cup) ground almonds
½ level teaspoon finely grated
orange peel
1 egg yolk
1 oz. (2T) butter
1 large glass sweet white wine
or Marsala

serves 4

Cover the peaches with boiling water and leave for 1 minute. Drain and cover with cold water. When cool enough to handle, lift the peaches out of the water and slide off the skins. Cut the peaches in half, remove the stones and place in a lightly buttered heatproof dish.
Combine the macaroon crumbs with the almonds and orange peel, then bind with the egg yolk. Spoon equal amounts into the peach cavities, then dot with flakes of butter.
Pour the wine into the dish. Cover and cook in a moderate oven (350°F, Mark 4) for 30 minutes. Serve while still warm.

Pesche alla cardinale   Cardinal peaches

4 oz. (1 cup) granulated sugar
¼ pint (⅝ cup) water
vanilla stick
4 peaches
1 breakfast cup (1 cup) raspberries, fresh or frozen
flaked almonds, toasted

First prepare a syrup by dissolving the sugar in the water. Add the vanilla stick, bring to the boil and boil steadily for about 5 minutes or until it becomes fairly thick and syrupy.

Prepare 4 peaches exactly as given in the previous recipe. Place the halved peaches, cut sides down, in a dish and coat with the hot syrup after first removing the vanilla stick. Cover and refrigerate when cold.

Before serving, crush the raspberries or blend to a purée in the blender. Remove the peaches from the syrup and transfer to 4 individual dishes. Coat with the raspberries, then sprinkle each with a few almonds.

note: the filled peaches may be served on ice cream as a Peach
serves 4   Melba.

Macedonia di frutta   Fruit salad

4 large Italian peaches
12 ripe apricots
juice of 1 lemon
1 small ripe melon
8 fresh figs
sugar
2 tablespoons (2½T) brandy

Cover the peaches and apricots with boiling water and leave for 1 minute. Drain and cover with cold water. When cool enough to handle, slide off the skins. Cut the fruit into slices and put into a serving bowl. Sprinkle with lemon juice to prevent discolouration. Cut the melon and figs into cubes and add to the bowl. Sprinkle with sugar and brandy and stir well to mix. Cover and refrigerate for about 4 hours.

note: plums, pineapple and other seasonal stone fruits may be
serves 4   added to the fruit salad as well.

Arance caramellate   Caramelized oranges

4 large oranges
8 oz. (1 cup) granulated sugar
½ pint (1¼ cups) water
1 tablespoon (1¼T) orange flavoured liqueur

Often served now in many Italian restaurants, these caramelized oranges are refreshing and sophisticated but at the same time easy to prepare and suitable for almost any occasion.

Peel the oranges carefully, removing all traces of white pith. Reserve the peel from two of the oranges and again cut away the white pith. Slice the peel into thin strips. Put the strips into a saucepan of cold water. Bring to the boil and boil slowly for 10 minutes or until tender. Drain.

Put the sugar into a saucepan with the water. Stir over a low heat until dissolved, then boil briskly until thickish and syrupy. Remove from the heat and leave to cool slightly. Stir in the liqueur.

Add the oranges to the pan of syrup and turn over and over until they are well-coated. Lift out of the pan and put on to a serving platter.

Add the orange peel strips to the remaining syrup in the pan. Cook gently until they begin to look transparent and the syrup itself turns pale gold. Pile equal amounts of peel and syrup on to each orange then chill thoroughly before serving.

note: these oranges are almost impossible to tackle with a spoon
serves 4   and fork so one is well advised to give everyone a dessert knife as well.

(following page) Peach melba (left)   Caramelized oranges (right)

Crema di mandorle con ciliege
Custard cream with nuts and cherries

6 eggs
1 pint (2½ cups) milk
3 level tablespoons (3¾T) castor (superfine) sugar
¼ teaspoon vanilla essence
½ pint (1¼ cups) double (heavy) cream
2 tablespoons (2½T) milk
12 cherries, halved
1 level tablespoon (1¼T) almonds, chopped and toasted

serves 4

Beat the eggs well. Bring the milk just up to the boil and combine with the eggs.

Add the sugar and vanilla and strain into a buttered heatproof dish of 2 to 2½ pint (5 to 6¼ cups) capacity. Stand in a roasting pan containing 2-inches of cold water. Cook in the centre of a cool oven (300°F, Mark 2) for 1½ hours or until the blade of a knife, inserted into the centre, comes out clean. Leave until cold then refrigerate until thoroughly chilled.

Before serving, turn the custard out on to a serving dish. Beat the cream and milk together until thick, then pile on top of the custard. Stud with the cherries, sprinkle with nuts and serve straight away.

note: if liked, marinate cherries overnight in 1 or 2 tablespoons (1¼–2½T) brandy.

Alternatively the custard cream may be served without the whipped cream topping, and simply decorated with cherries and angelica.

Monte Bianco Chestnut Monte Bianco

12 oz. (3 cups) dried chestnuts, soaked overnight
6 oz. (¾ cup) castor (superfine) sugar
½ teaspoon vanilla essence
pinch of salt
2 dessertspoons (2T) rum
¼ pint (⅝ cup) double (heavy) cream
1 tablespoon (1¼T) milk
sifted icing (confectioners') sugar
2 level tablespoons (2½T) grated plain chocolate
serves 4

Put the drained chestnuts into a saucepan and cover with cold water. Bring to the boil, cover and simmer gently until very tender; about 30 to 40 minutes. Drain thoroughly and mash finely with a fork. Stir in the sugar, essence, salt and half the rum. Press the chestnut mixture through a colander or sieve—with coarse holes—directly into a small serving bowl, allowing it to fall freely into a mound. Beat the cream and milk together until softly stiff, then stir in the rest of the rum and icing (confectioners') sugar to taste. Spoon over the chestnut mixture, then sprinkle with the chocolate. Serve straight away.

Granita al caffè Coffee granita

1 pint (2½ cups) very strong hot coffee
2 oz. (¼ cup) granulated sugar

The granita is a cross between a sorbet and a water ice and during the height of summer—or after a heavy meal—is one of the most refreshing desserts in existence. Granita is, basically, half frozen crystals of ice, sweetened and flavoured to taste and served in small glasses. Easy and uncomplicated to make, any granita tastes impressive and does much to stimulate a flagging digestion.

Combine the coffee and sugar well together and stir until the sugar dissolves.
Pour into 1 or 2 empty ice cube trays and leave in the freezing compartment of the refrigerator until half frozen; between 2 to 3 hours. Stir the granita every hour while it is freezing to break down the ice crystals.

serves 4

Spoon into glasses and serve quickly as it melts fast.

Granita di limone Lemon granita

6 oz. (¾ cup) granulated sugar
¾ pint (2 cups) water
juice of 4 large lemons
peel of 1 lemon, finely grated
serves 4

Dissolve the sugar in the water.
Leave until cold then stir in the juice of the lemons and the finely grated peel.
Freeze as directed in caffè granita but allow a little more time as the extra sugar slows up the freezing process.

Granita di arancia Orange granita

juice of 2 large lemons
juice of 2 medium oranges
peel of 1 orange, finely grated

Make exactly as above.

Granita di agrumi Mixed citrus granita

juice of 2 large lemons
juice of 1 large orange
juice of 1 medium grapefruit
1 level teaspoon finely grated grapefruit peel

Make exactly as limone granita.

For a subtle and interesting flavour, add a few leaves of fresh mint to the hot syrup but remove these once the syrup is cold.

Custard cream (left)

Chestnut Monte Bianco (following page)

Ice cream

True Italian home-made ice cream—doubtless the best anywhere—is based on an egg and milk custard, flavoured to taste with vanilla, coffee, chocolate or whatever, sweetened with sugar and then frozen. When whipped cream is added as well, the ice cream becomes sugar-smooth and utterly luxurious with a texture and flavour of remarkable quality. It would be unfair to say that this type of ice cream requires no attention. On the contrary, it needs loving care, a lot of patience and very fresh ingredients. But the effort is well worthwhile, for it is as different from commercially made ice cream as chalk from cheese. To prevent food in the refrigerator cabinet from freezing, turn the control back to normal setting once the ice cream is firm.

Gelato di vaniglia — Vanilla ice cream

¾ pint (2 cups) single (coffee) cream
6 egg yolks
6 oz. (¾ cup) vanilla sugar
¼ pint (⅝ cup) double (heavy) cream

serves 6

Set the refrigerator control to the coldest setting at least 1 hour before making the ice cream.
Heat the cream slowly, stirring continuously, until it just comes to the boil.
Remove from the heat and pour into a basin standing over a saucepan of gently boiling water. Beat in the egg yolks and sugar. Cook, stirring frequently, until the mixture thickens sufficiently to coat the back of a spoon, but do not allow the custard to boil or it will curdle.
Remove from the heat, leave until cool, then strain into 2 empty ice cube trays. Cover each with foil, then stand the trays in the freezing compartment of the refrigerator.
Leave until the ice cream has frozen about ½-inch round the sides of the trays, then tip into a bowl and beat briskly until the mixture is smooth. Return to trays, cover with foil and freeze until half frozen. Tip into the bowl as before and beat briskly until smooth.
Whip the cream until softly stiff then fold the custard mixture into it. Put into trays and freeze for about 2½ hours or until firm.

Gelato di caffè — Coffee ice cream

Make exactly as vanilla ice cream but heat the cream slowly with 2 level tablespoons (2½T) medium ground coffee and strain. Use ordinary castor (superfine) sugar instead of vanilla sugar.

Gelato di cioccolate — Chocolate ice cream

Make exactly as vanilla ice cream but melt 3 oz. (3 squares) bitter chocolate slowly in the cream. Include vanilla sugar but reduce the amount by 1 oz. (⅛ cup).

Gelato di nocciolini — Hazelnut ice cream

Make exactly as vanilla ice cream but stir in 2 to 3 level tablespoons (2½–3¾T) very finely chopped hazelnuts at the same time as the whipped cream.

Gelato di limone — Lemon ice cream

Make exactly as vanilla ice cream but stir in the finely grated peel of 1 medium lemon at the same time as the whipped cream.

Gelato di lamponi — Raspberry ice cream

½ pint (1¼ cups) double (heavy) cream
½ pint (1¼ cups) thick raspberry purée, made from frozen or fresh raspberries
4 oz. (½ cup) castor (superfine) sugar

serves 6

Set the refrigerator control to the coldest setting at least 1 hour before making the ice cream. Beat the cream and sugar together until thick, then gently fold the raspberry purée into it. Transfer to 1 or 2 empty ice cube trays, cover with foil and freeze for 1 hour.
Tip into a bowl, break up with a fork and return to the trays. Freeze for a further hour. Tip into the bowl and beat with a fork until smooth. Return to the trays, cover with foil and freeze for about 2 to 3 hours or until firm.

Gelato di fragole — Strawberry ice cream

Make exactly as raspberry ice cream, using thick strawberry purée instead of the raspberry.

Gelato di albicocche — Apricot ice cream

Make exactly as raspberry ice cream, using thick apricot purée instead of raspberry. A level teaspoon of finely grated orange peel improves the flavour.

125

A selection of ice creams (left)

(previous page) Chocolate ice cream (left)

Vanilla ice cream (right)

Cheese

Italy offers us a surprisingly generous range of dessert and cooking cheeses which have their own distinctive characters. Regrettably many of the cheeses—some made in the countryside by local farmers, others produced on a commercial basis—must be consumed fresh and, therefore, are unsuitable for export. Those that are, however, are listed below in our small 'dictionary' and should give you some idea of what is generally available in Italian food shops and supermarkets.

I formaggi Cheese

Bel Paese—or 'Beautiful Country'—is a very well known and popular cheese made in the north of Italy, near Milan. It is a gentle cheese with a delicate flavour and soft, creamy texture and makes an excellent table or dessert cheese. It keeps well and because of its melting properties, may also be used in cooking instead of Mozzarella.

Burrini is a firm, well-flavoured cheese from the south with a large piece of butter inside it. When cut, each slice consists of a ring of cheese encircling a round of creamy butter which, for some reason best known to itself, stays beautifully fresh. This cheese is fun to serve and eat and makes a good lunch or supper snack with crusty bread or rolls.

Dolcelatte: This is a mild, delicate and creamy cheese with green veining. It is less impressive, perhaps, than Gorgonzola, but well-liked by those who find stronger cheeses overwhelming.

Fontina: Used for the famous Piedmont Fonduta—the Italian version of Fondue—this is a rich and creamy cheese with a distinctive flavour. In appearance, it looks rather like Gruyère but has smaller holes. Sometimes it is served as a dessert cheese.

Gorgonzola is to the Italians what Stilton is to the British and Roquefort to the French. A superior and exquisitely flavoured fairly strong cheese with a soft, creamy texture and turquoise coloured veining. It is made in the North of Italy and was first produced in the 9th century.

Mozzarella: This is a soft, mild and pliable cheese, best eaten very fresh and still moist with its own whey. When dry, it serves best as a cooking cheese and is frequently used as a topping for pizza. At one time, Mozzarella was made only from buffalo's milk but, due to a shortage of buffaloes, cow's milk has tended to replace it. Connoisseurs claim that Mozzarella made with buffalo's milk has a better flavour, but this is a matter of opinion.

Parmesan: It would be hard to imagine a pasta dish without the

traditional hint of Parmesan, and indeed this famous cheese is
probably more widely used than any other in the cuisine of Italy.
It has an unmistakable, pungent flavour with a slight bite, is pale
creamy-yellow in colour and has a close, grainy and almost rocky
texture; hence the name 'Grana' by which Parmesan is known in
Italy. It is an age-old cheese produced in the Northern regions and
has been in existence almost 1,000 years, although the people of
Parma insist it is much older still. Certainly, Parmesan has always
played an important part in Italian cooking and when mature (at
least two years old), makes an excellent dessert cheese with a glass
of full-bodied red Chianti. Mostly Parmesan cheese is sold in tubs,
already grated and quite expensive. A more economical way is to buy
a piece of Parmesan and do it yourself, grating only as much as is
required for immediate use; like coffee, Parmesan loses flavour and
aroma if grated in bulk and then stored for any length of time. It is
useful to know that in the piece, Parmesan keeps almost
indefinitely and improves greatly with age.

Pecorino: This is a hard, fairly strong cheese made from sheep's
milk. It is found throughout Italy and is often used in cooking
instead of Parmesan. Table Pecorino is milder than the cooking
variety and makes an excellent dessert cheese either on its own or
accompanied by crisp apples or ripe pears.

Provolone: This is a flavoursome cheese made from buffalo's or cow's
milk and comes in various sizes and assorted shapes. When fresh and
still soft it may be eaten as a dessert cheese. When older and harder
it is excellent for cooking. Sometimes this cheese is smoked and is
then known as Provolone Affumicato.

Ricotta is a smooth white and bland cheese—mild and slightly
sweet—which could be bracketed with the Quark of Germany, the
Demi-Sel of France and the Cottage Cheese of the U.S.A. and
Britain. It is a by-product of other cheeses and, in Italy, is often used
as a sweet and savoury cooking ingredient and sometimes as a
dessert cheese.

Wines

In a country which flows with vast quantities of every conceivable wine imaginable—and fine wine at that—is it any wonder that those who have visited Italy come away with a feeling of La Dolce Vita and, in retrospect, the firm belief that 'In vino veritas!'* Sadly, not all the wines take well to travel and this is said with a measure of disappointment for many of the local ones—too sensitive to be moved far—are a poem and one would dearly love to enjoy them in the leisure of one's own home. Be that as it may, some excellent wines from all over Italy are exported and listed below are the ones that should be obtainable from wine merchants and supermarkets without too much difficulty.

*Truth comes out in wine—Pliny—AD 23–79

I vini italiani   Wines of Italy

Chianti: Everyone is familiar with Chianti, the famous red or white Italian wine in its raffia-covered bulbous bottle which is made, in enormous quantities, in north-west Italy, in the province of Tuscany. Chianti, usually drunk while still young (about six months), is an everyday table wine of reasonable merit and teams happily with robust and earthy foods, with coarse sausage, with strong cheese and crusty bread. Chianti Classico, however, is produced in smaller amounts near Sienna (and carries the official government stamp in the form of a yellow seal) and is a wine of greater character, quality and maturity than ordinary Chianti, primarily because it is produced more individually on specific estates and allowed to mature for several years before being sold. Most of the Chianto Classico is red, although a small quantity of white is also available.

Barolo: A wine from Piedmont in the extreme north-west of Italy. Full-bodied, red and heavy with a rich, aromatic bouquet, it is considered to be one of the finest wines in the world. Like vintage Burgundy, it should be reserved for beef roasts and grills.

Barbaresco: Also from the Piedmont region comes Barbaresco, a lighter wine than Barolo and less heavily scented. It, too, is a suitable wine for beef dishes and roasts in particular.

Barbera: Yet another wine from Piedmont is Barbera, completely different in character from the Barolo and Barbaresco and considerably less mellow. This is a lighter, slightly more acid wine, usually served open in the carafe. Barbera is a good quality wine but not in the same class as Barolo and Barbaresco.

Valpolicella: Valpolicella comes from the Venice area and is a light dry red wine with charm and character. It has a good bouquet and flavour and is at its best slightly chilled. Delightful, in fact, to sip during long summer evenings or to serve with simple pasta dishes.

Soave di Verona: This is an intriguing white wine, light, dry, fresh and pale. Usually bottled in long, green bottles which are similar to those used for the famous German Moselle, it is Italy's best wine and comes from the village Soave, north-east of Verona. It is excellent with fish.

Lacrima Christi: This is a wine which comes from the slopes of mount Vesuvius and is usually golden in colour and fairly sweet. Other varieties of the same wine are red and dry.

Orvieto: Orvieto is a white wine from the province of Umbria. It has a subtle sweetness which is neither cloying nor rich and is a smooth, light wine with a faintly aromatic bouquet. A perfect dessert wine, especially with nuts and summer fruits.

Frascati: Named after the town of Frascati which is close to Rome, Frascati comes from the Alban hills and is a full-bodied, strong white wine with a pleasant fragrance. It is honey-coloured and dry.

Asti Spumante: Asti Spumante—from the region of Piedmont—is a sparkling, sweet white wine which is the Italian equivalent of French champagne and German Sekt. It is a gay and heady wine, suitable for serving with the dessert course at the end of a meal. It also makes a pleasant drink on its own with sweet nibbles of biscuits, dates, glacé fruits and nuts.

Marsala: This is a Sicilian wine which has been enjoyed by the British for some two hundred years. It is a rich wine, similar in many ways to a mature sherry, and was first shipped to Britain in 1773 by an Englishman called John Woodhouse. Today there are three categories of Marsala available which vary in quality, price and flavour. Virgin Marsala is the least sweet, the best quality and the most expensive. Next comes Garibaldi and then Italia, which is highly commendable as a cooking wine and additive to clear soups. Marsala enjoys the reputation of being Italy's finest dessert wine— which it is—but also makes an excellent aperitif.

(previous page) Gorgonzola (left)   *Bordolino vineyards (above right)*

Chianti (right)   *Vats for Ruffino Chianti (right)*

Gli aperitivi   Aperitifs

Vermouths The most famous Italian aperitif is Vermouth which is produced mainly in Turin but also locally in other parts of the country. It is a blend of wine made from Muscat grapes, fortified and distilled with an assortment of some fifty herbs, the principal one being wormwood (or the German Wermut, from which the drink is named). Vermouth may be either white (bianco) or red (rosso) and either sweet or dry.

Bitters Also popular as aperitifs are Italian bitters made from a secret combination of herbs, spirits and, in some cases, quinine. They are an acquired taste—too bitter for many—and include vivid red Campari—nearly always served with ice, soda and a twist of orange—Punt e Mes containing quinine, Cynar made from artichokes and also quinine and Chinato which has, as its base, Barolo wine and Fernet Branca.

Entertaining

Because there is a big selection of interesting and colourful dishes to suit almost any occasion and please even the most discerning palates, Italian food lends itself admirably to either informal or formal entertaining. The Italians themselves are hospitable and warm-hearted people and enjoy having guests, either to share their bowl of spaghetti or outsize pizza and bottle of Chianti or, at the other end of the scale, to sit down more formally to a three course lunch or dinner with all the trimmings and appropriate wines.

Below are our menu suggestions for winter and summer. Each consists of three courses and the quantities of ingredients listed in all the recipes should be doubled, trebled or even quadrupled depending on the number of guests invited.

Dinner or Lunch Summer

Rice salad	(page 13)
Grilled sole	(page 68)
Cucumber salad with fennel	(page 104)

Fresh seasonal fruit or if
cheese is preferred, Ricotta
with biscuits and butter
Coffee
Wine: Frascati or
Soave di Verona

Parma ham with melon	(page 23)
Fried chicken with tomatoes and pimentos	(page 93)
Green bean salad	(page 109)
Apricot ice cream	(page 125)

or fresh seasonal fruit. If
cheese is preferred,
Dolcelatte with biscuits and
butter
Coffee
Wine: Frascati or
Soave di Verona

Stracciatella	(page 32)
Ham pizza	(page 57)
Lettuce salad	(page 104)
Strawberry ice cream	(page 125)

or fresh seasonal fruit. If
cheese is preferred, Bel Paese
with biscuits and butter
Coffee
Wine: Valpolicella or
Barbera

Egg and tuna mayonnaise	(page 20)
Cannelloni	(page 49)
Tomato salad	(page 108)
Pesche alla cardinale	(page 113)

or if cheese is preferred, table
Pecorino with biscuits
and butter
Coffee
Wine: Valpolicella or Barbera

Dinner or Lunch Summer

Garlic dressed artichoke hearts	(page 17)
Fritto misto mare	(page 66)
Mixed salad	(page 105)
Arancia granita or	(page 117)

fresh seasonal fruit.
If cheese is preferred,
Burrini with biscuits
Coffee
Wine: Frascati or
Soave di Verona

Dressed beans	(page 12)
Vitello tonnato	(page 77)
Lettuce salad	(page 104)
Fruit salad or if cheese is preferred, Gorgonzola with biscuits and butter	(page 113)

Coffee
Wine: Frascati or
Soave di Verona

Dinner or Lunch winter

Artichokes with mayonnaise	(page 16)
Chicken cacciatora	(page 89)
Fried courgettes (zucchini)	(page 98)
Zabaglione	(page 112)

or if cheese is preferred,
Dolcelatte with biscuits
and butter
Coffee
Wine: Soave di Verona or
Frascati

Semolina gnocchi	(page 57)
Boiled fish with garlic sauce	(page 69)
Boiled potatoes	
Tomato salad	(page 108)

Fresh seasonal fruit, or if
cheese is preferred,
Gorgonzola with biscuits
and butter
Coffee
Wine: Barbera or
Frascati

(following page)

Peppers, Italian style (1)

Egg-laced soup (2)

Fish shop window display in Venice (3)

Veal escalopes with Marsala (4)

Semolina gnocchi (5)

Stuffed peaches in wine (6)

Dinner or Lunch winter

Hot cheese antipasto (page 12)
L'osso buco (page 77)
Risotto Milanese (page 52)
Caramelized oranges (page 113)
or if cheese is preferred, fresh
Provolone with biscuits
and butter
Coffee
Wine: Soave di Verona or
Frascati

Zuppa di lentecchie (page 28)
Beef stoffato (page 81)
Pasta al burro (page 38)
Green vegetables to taste
Zabaglione (page 112)
or if cheese is preferred, table
Pecorino with biscuits
and butter
Coffee
Wine: Barbaresco, Barbera or
Valpolicella

Milanese style minestrone (page 25)
Roast duck (page 95)
Crumbed potato cakes (page 99)
Green vegetables to taste
Fresh seasonal fruit or if
cheese is preferred, Burrini
with biscuits
Coffee
Wine: Barolo or Barberesco

Stuffed aubergines with egg (page 9)
Roast lamb with Marsala (page 78)
Fried potatoes with rosemary (page 100)
Creamed spinach (page 100)
Chestnut Monte Bianco (page 117)
or if cheese is preferred,
Bel paese with biscuits
and butter
Coffee
Wine: Barolo or Barberesco

Parties hot

Bagna cauda (page 21)
Seafood salad with mushrooms (page 109)
Cauliflower salad (page 104)
Tomato salad (page 108)
Cold escalopes (page 74)
Fruit salad and/or (page 113)
Chocolate ice cream (page 125)
Various cheeses, butter
and biscuits
Coffee
Wine: Valpolicella and
Frascati or Orvieto if sweet
white wine is preferred

Parties cold

Brodo con farfallo (page 32)
Risi e bisi (page 54)
Fried scampi with (page 66)
Salsa verde (page 71)
Small pizza (page 57)
Dressed beans (page 12)
Stuffed peaches in wine (page 112)
Various cheeses, biscuits
and butter
Coffee
Wine: Barbera and Frascati,
Asti Spumante if liked

Weights & Measures

All recipes in this book are based on Imperial weights and measures, with American equivalents in parenthesis.
Measures in weight in the Imperial and American systems are the same. Measures in volume are different, and the following table shows the equivalents:

spoon measures: level spoon measurements are used throughout.

Imperial	American
1 teaspoon (5 ml)	$1\frac{1}{4}$ teaspoons
1 tablespoon (20 ml)	$1\frac{1}{4}$ tablespoons (abbrev.: T)

liquid measures:

Imperial	American	
20 fluid oz.	16 fluid oz.	1 pint
10 fluid oz.	8 fluid oz.	1 cup

Metric measures

The following table shows both an exact conversion from Imperial to metric measures and the recommended working equivalent.

weight:

Imperial oz.	metric grams	working equivalent grams
1	28·35	25
2	56·7	50
4	113·4	100
8	226·8	200
12	340·2	300
1·0 lb.	453	400
1·1 lb.	$\frac{1}{2}$ kilo	
2·2 lb.	1 kilo	

liquid measures:

Imperial	exact conversion	working equivalent
$\frac{1}{4}$ pint (1 gill)	142 millilitres	150 ml.
$\frac{1}{2}$ pint	284 ml.	300 ml.
1 pint	568 ml.	600 ml.
$1\frac{3}{4}$ pints	994 ml.	1 litre

linear measures:

1 inch	$2\frac{1}{2}$ cm.
2 inch	5 cm.
3 inch	$7\frac{1}{2}$ cm.
6 inch	15 cm.

It is useful to note for easy reference that: 1 kilogramme (1000 grammes) = 2·2 lb. therefore $\frac{1}{2}$ kilo (500 grammes) roughly = 1 lb.
1 litre roughly = $1\frac{3}{4}$ imperial pints therefore $\frac{1}{2}$ litre roughly = imperial pints

Oven temperatures

In this book oven temperatures are given in degrees Fahrenheit with the equivalent Gas mark number. The following chart gives the conversions from degrees Fahrenheit to degrees Centigrade:

°F	°C	
225	110	very cool or very slow
250	130	
275	140	cool or slow
300	150	
325	170	very moderate
350	180	moderate
375	190	moderately hot
400	200	
425	220	hot
450	230	very hot
475	240	

Index

Figures in italics refer to illustrations.

Acknowledgments

The following black and white photographs by courtesy of:

ARGENTINE BEEF BUREAU   p. 88
BARNABY PICTURE LIBRARY   p. 17, step a; p. 68, a, b, c; p. 70, top
BERTORELLI   p. 124
BRITISH EGG INFORMATION
SERVICE   p. 59; p. 60; p. 61; p. 111; p. 112
CADBURY SCHWEPPES FOOD
ADVISORY SERVICE   p. 29
CAMERA PRESS   p. 8; p. 16, bottom; p. 18; p. 31; p. 53; p. 64; p. 66; p. 70, bottom; p. 76; p. 101; p. 108
CONWAY PICTURE LIBRARY   p. 12; p. 13; p. 16, top; p. 17, steps b & c; p. 19; p. 24; p. 26; p. 27; p. 28; p. 37, a & b; p. 38; p. 49; p. 50; p. 51; p. 55; p. 56; p. 58; p. 89; p. 99; p. 106–107; p. 120–121
CORDON BLEU   p. 79
FINDUS   p. 65; p. 92
FLOUR ADVISORY BUREAU   p. 85
FRATELLI FABBRI EDITORE   p. 63
HEDGES AND BUTLER LTD
(picture by Dmitre Kasterine)   p. 132, top; p. 132–133, bottom
INTERNATIONAL DISTILLERS AND
VINTNERS   p. 128
PAF INTERNATIONAL   p. 23; p. 103
PASTA FOODS LIMITED   p. 34
PHOTOPAD   p. 110
SYNDICATION INTERNATIONAL   p. 4; p. 72–73; p. 78; p. 80; p. 96–97; p. 105; p. 116
TABASCO SAUCE   p. 43; p. 47

The following colour transparencies by courtesy of:

BARNABY PICTURE LIBRARY   p. 40; p. 130; p. 138, 3; p. 142–143
CONWAY PICTURE LIBRARY   p. 10
CORDON BLEU   p. 94, top
FRATELLI FABBRI EDITORE   p. 15, bottom; p. 48; p. 82, bottom right; p. 114; p. 118–119; p. 123; p. 126; p. 131; p. 138, 4; p. 139, 6
GALBANI   p. 127
JOHN WEST FOODS LIMITED   p. 14; p. 86
LAWRY'S FOODS INC.   p. 41; p. 44, bottom; p. 83
PAF INTERNATIONAL   p. 11, top; p. 11 bottom right; p. 87, bottom; p. 90, above; p. 95
PASTA FOODS LIMITED   p. 6–7
PENTANGLE PHOTOGRAPHY   p. 2–3; p. 87, top; p. 91, bottom; p. 138, 2
PHOTOPAD   p. 11, bottom left; p. 15, top; p. 33; p. 45; p. 82, bottom left; p. 94, bottom; p. 115; p. 135; p. 138, 1
SYNDICATION INTERNATIONAL   p. 36; p. 44, top; p. 45, bottom; p. 82; p. 91, top; p. 139, 5
TABASCO SAUCE   p. 90, bottom
WALLS ICE CREAM   p. 122